Awen Publications (founded in Bath in 2003) publishes poetry, fiction, and literary non-fiction, with an ecobardic focus. Our mission is to match quality of writing with an engagement with the world.

'*All real poetry seeks to "renew the face of the earth" – and so to resist the exploiting, banalization or defacing of what lies around us. I hope this collection will serve the renewal we so badly need.*'

Most Revd Dr Rowan Williams

'*Soul of the Earth is for those who care about the Earth, those who are keeping the flame of optimism for the future burning in your heart. This is a collection of beautifully crafted poems by poets from around the world.*'

Cygnus Community Review

Also from Awen Publications:

Poetry

Places of Truth: journeys into sacred wilderness by Jay Ramsay
Iona by Mary Palmer
Tidal Shift: selected poems by Mary Palmer
Silver Branch by Kevan Manwaring
The Immanent Moment by Kevan Manwaring
Signature of Kisses by Simon Miles
Dancing with Dark Goddesses: movements in poetry by Irina Kuzminsky
Crackle of Almonds: selected poems by Gabriel Bradford Miller
Glossing the Spoils by Charlotte Hussey

Fiction

Exotic Excursions by Anthony Nanson
The Firekeeper's Daughter by Karola Renard
The Long Woman by Kevan Manwaring
Windsmith by Kevan Manwaring
The Well under the Sea by Kevan Manwaring
The Burning Path by Kevan Manwaring
This Fearful Tempest by Kevan Manwaring

Non-fiction

An Ecobardic Manifesto: a vision for the arts in a time of environmental crisis
    by Fire Springs
Words of Re-enchantment: writings on storytelling, myth, and ecological desire
    by Anthony Nanson

Mixed forms

The Fifth Quarter by Richard Selby
Mysteries by Chrissy Derbyshire
Writing the Land: an anthology of natural words edited by Kevan Manwaring

SOUL

OF THE EARTH

The Awen Anthology of Eco-spiritual Poetry

edited by Jay Ramsay

AWEN
Stroud

First published by Awen Publications 2010
This edition published 2016 by Awen Publications
12 Belle Vue Close, Stroud, GL5 1ND, England
www.awenpublications.co.uk

ISBN 978-1-906900-17-5

Cover image: *Earth – Apollo 17. Full Earth Showing Africa and Antarctica*.
Copyright © NASA 1972. Apollo 17 hand-held Hasselblad picture of the
full Earth. This picture was taken on 7 December 1972, as the spacecraft
travelled to the moon on the last of the Apollo missions. A remarkably
cloud-free Africa is at upper left, stretching down to the centre of the im-
age. Saudi Arabia is visible at the top of the disc and Antarctica and the
South Pole are at the bottom. Asia is on the horizon at upper right. The
Earth is 12,740 km in diameter. (Apollo 17, AS17-148-22727)

Originally published with support from Cyprus Well
& Hurtwood Ltd Energy Consultancy

Production by Wordsmith Communication and Awen Publications

in memory of Mary Palmer (1957–2009)
poet, radical Christian, sister, friend

and this shoal gathered here
for poetry and true love-life-freedom

The gentle touch of wave and silt
and silence
                    shimmered me
smoked pink: an iridescence you, no doubt,
would have microscoped down to grey
specks on cold flesh
                    but a shoal gathered
able to see, understand and believe in
a salmon that swims free.

Mary Palmer

To be awake is to be alive. I've never met a man who was quite awake. How would I look him in the face?

Henry David Thoreau

If we choose to let conjecture run wild, the animals all partake of our origin in one common ancestor ... we may all be netted together.

Charles Darwin

CONTENTS

INTRODUCTION

Imagine for a moment it's you, floating there in space, looking down, all seeing eye, and seeing for the first time the Earth as it is in its created reality ... seeing it as Edgar Mitchell did. What do you see in its glowing blueness with its swathes of cloud, sea, and continents blending and interfusing? What does it mean for you? Can you remember the first time you saw this image, and the impact it had on you? The soul of a thing is visible to the naked eye. What we're seeing is the Soul of the Earth.

There's no need to spell out any more where we're at. What was still debated as hypothesis among the scientific community in the late 1990s when I edited my previous eco-spiritual anthology, *Earth Ascending*, is now common knowledge – except among those still rigorously in denial. Knowledge that the planet itself is busy broadcasting in its telluric shifting and its weather systems. There actually is nowhere to hide, except by looking nowhere; but everywhere we do look we're starting to see the same thing: the boiling points of humanity and environment are the same thing, the one mirroring the other. 'Koyaanisquatsi', as the Hopi said, meaning 'the resulting state of things'.

Change is the inevitable alchemy; both inner and outer (it can't be one or the other). As Martin Palmer, religious adviser to the UN, put it succinctly in his foreword to *Earth Ascending*:

> The crises which affect us and our world are not crises of resources. It is not ultimately a crisis of the planet. It is a crisis of our hearts and minds. No solution will be found outside ourselves and our visions, beliefs, hopes and fears. No great government schemes, international projects or endless conferences will change anything unless and until we have changed our hearts and minds.

What isn't perhaps so clear for us is to see the opportunity the crisis is revealing. (In Chinese wisdom, the ideogram for 'crisis' also means 'opportunity'.) For that we have to see the situation not just environmentally (or concretely), but spiritually and to some extent abstractly as well. Hence the hyphenation 'eco-spiritual' – it has to be both. It really is all gloom and doom otherwise.

Change is the opportunity – to move, within ourselves, from the primacy of gut reaction and judgement to the heart, our centre of true feeling, which connects us to one another and enables us to go beyond ourselves, beyond our self-preoccupation, into the bigger picture. We cannot change the planet until we can think – as we are starting to – 'as One', beyond the barriers that still divide us. Those walls in our 'rigged reality' (as Niall McDevitt puts it) have been coming down and must continue to come down. At the same time, this work is also interpersonal and is taking place in every community everywhere – the same East End street of our daily life, all our many little dramas in which our own process is transparent (increasingly) within a shared language of honesty.

So as I sat on the Eurostar to Brussels, to take part in 'Tools of the Sacred; Techniques of the Secular', an international poetry conference organised by Franca Bellarsi, and overheard a guy talking on a mobile about how 'a volcano is working against you', I didn't know whether to laugh (he was quite serious) or take him to task. I did neither: I wrote it down. A few hours later, the conference hotel was teeming with activity, with ecology firmly on the agenda in a way I couldn't have imagined ... and the seed for this book was planted when I met the Seattle-based poet Paul Nelson. There was lots of talk, quite rightly, about Gary Snyder, now an elder statesman, and his evocation of the preservation of nature as 'the central moral imperative of our age' – beyond the tedious contractions of nihilism, which seemed disappointingly English by comparison. There was little mention of Ted Hughes, who was surely on the case in the 1970s; and of course there was little or no mention of *this* generation of committed poets, now in their prime, who are busy combining spiritual awareness, values, and faith with ecological expression.

Many positive things emerged from that conference, reflected also in the arrangement of quotations above; but one thing was memorable, expressed in so many ways: the emergence of a new universality which literature, and poetry perhaps especially, can play a vital role in witnessing and awakening. Another was that to accomplish the shift that's required (as Arne Næss has said) we must spend time in Nature. We must be *in* what we're talking about, just as we need to be in our physical bodies and our senses (all six of them) if we are to appreciate the gift and opportunity of life, moment by moment. All the many facets of disconnection become obvious when you see this; as does the way the call of intimate relationship and the call of the earth are (as Kevan Manwaring celebrates here in 'Breaking Light') revealed to be part of the same thing.

At the same time, the 'Soul of the World' (or Anima Mundi) contains a collective knowing that doesn't leave us alone; it surrounds us and informs our dreams. Yeats always testified to this. Even in Disney World, the Tree of Life (Yggdrasil) appears, all creatures intertwined in its roots. We know this deep within ourselves – that's the implication. So what we do for the planet we do because we are part of it. What we *don't* do is the consequence of our loss of connection, stranded in our separated egos. Connection is where crisis transforms into opportunity, experienced as awakening and return to being – 'inside the skin of things', as I put it in my Chrysalis poetry course. We become 'I', our authentic selves, rooted in our hearts and the deeper wildness as the men and women we truly are.

In the psychology of More to Life (originating in the United States), we have a line that separates *connecting* thoughts above from *separating* thoughts below. Below the line we have fear, early decisions, denial, expectation, judgement; above the line: noticing, truthtelling, choosing, creating, and gratitude. Literally, two worlds, a vortex reaching either side. We might literally say Heaven and Hell, or (as Jesus did) 'the kingdom of heaven is within you'. The paradox is that we live in both worlds; however, the crux is that we can *keep choosing* to go above the line.

In the powerful experiential seminars of Be the Change (seeded among the Indians of the Amazon rainforest), after being asked, 'What are the two greatest challenges facing the world?' we are asked, 'What gives you hope? What are you grateful for?' It's the same orientation and emphasis, which also reveals that truly positive thinking (rather than the shallow 'positivity' of denial) is essential and is where we'll find and free the spirit in our minds. At the same time, in what Joanna Macy calls 'the great turning', we can't wake up unless we wake up *as a group* – another level of understanding community, which includes how we see ourselves as artists and writers. Individuality remains vital, but the solo egoic journey that is essentially separative is not what we need. Years ago, Sri Aurobindo asked the question, if evolution were *only* to produce another Beethoven or Schubert or Mozart, where actually would we be going?

What can bring people into Love? What can release people's passion and commitment? Those are the questions we need to be asking to change the dream of our culture rather than to reconfirm its negativity, its self-fulfilling prophecy. When we are surrounded by challenge on so many levels (financially too, now), we start to see what the significance of the choice is. We are being asked, individually and collectively, to make an absolutely basic spiritual choice for life. We must be committed to consistently making this choice, instead of throwing in the towel. It's worth remembering that, for anyone likely to be reading this book, more than eighty per cent of the world is worse off than you. 'It's really hard right now. For everybody,' says Paul Hawken (of Be the Change). Somewhere within our collective suffering is our collective rebirth. Within our suffering too is the potential to name the very mindsets that keep us there: things like 'We have a right to use everything because it exists,' 'It's not my problem,' 'We are all alone,' 'I'm more important than you are,' 'What I do won't make any difference,' 'If I stand out, I will be persecuted.' At the same time: *Whatever I do to you, I do to me.* Who can deny it? We all live on an island we can't leave … despite our fantasies of unlimited space exploration.

So, while we live in 'blessed unrest', as Be the Change says, 'the power of one is the power to do something'; and if we play our part our life will have meaning. Faith is revealed as a place where I am beyond the trouble of what I feel; not a place of certainty, but a surrender to trusting that whatever 'is' is possibly also for the best. It is beyond my mind, beyond my doubt. What separates me from my faith is not being present, not being here, and so not allowing *the* Presence which Rumi's poetry evokes. It's the same call to Life, we realise, from every direction and to a new experience of the Divine as immanent within all of this.

Healing is part of this call and an essential part of how effective we can be in all there is to do at this time. It's not a fluffy sentimental thing; it really is about our own empowerment – and, as many of us feel, the sense that we are not quite living all we came here to be. Healing requires this level of honesty, that we become congruent as people (walking our talk), and that we learn to listen to the inner guidance that is always with us … which we secretly fear will humiliate us. Sickness is what happens when we don't follow our intuition. As Caroline Myss points out in *Defy Gravity*, the mind is afraid to heal, but the soul is not. Ego and soul must be brought together. 'People don't heal because they don't make it to the sacred,' as she put it in a lecture. This is where change and surrender become part of the same process, surrender to the mystical laws that go beyond our will. Listening to our intuition becomes absolutely vital; it becomes the golden thread. Where is my soul today? What are my choices? Are they inspired by fear or courage? As a client of mine said recently, 'I realise it's not about what makes me happy; it's about what makes me bigger as a person.'

All of these issues are present within the awareness of the poets gathered in this anthology: most of them known to me personally; some whose work I included in previous anthologies like *Angels of Fire* and *Transformation*, going back over twenty years now. These are voices in their prime, over half of them female. What is so remarkable about these poems in the midst of the situation we are in *is* their brightness, their truly positive energy, their embodied transformation. Again and again it is this quality of spiritual strength that shines through, born of knowing the absolute preciousness of life itself, with 'us the most fleeting of all', as Rilke phrased it. Paradoxically, this very awareness of transience reveals what is transcendent and exists within the fabric of our being as human beings who are connected and in relationship. That is what this poetry testifies to;

these are the poems I had to choose.

As Martin went on to say (and Blake as well as Shelley would have gladly echoed), 'It's only when the poets have made us look again, inward and outward, that we shall see our way.' I hope these poems speak as clearly and inspiringly to you, wherever you are sitting reading this, as the world goes on all around us in its daylight and its Dark Night, and the Soul of the Earth holds us in so many more ways than we know.

Jay Ramsay

ROSELLE ANGWIN

Day Lilies

Fierce, dressed to spill in flame, tangerine, melon-yellow
in their wide cobalt pots by the stone barn where the black

Asian pig scoffed my banana skin in one undershot gulp
without lifting her bulk from the straw, at dawn where swifts

threshed the sky. That month, July, the sun burnt hotter in this
heating-up globe but that day it didn't and anyway I didn't mind,

I forgot my fear for the planet and all of us and smiled and scratched
the pig's wire-brush back and lifted my face to the salt-charged breeze

just lipping the edge of the Fleet with its snow of swans.
That morning I'd read in a book on cosmology 'Every pair of planets

creates a single dance'. Around us the sky whirled. Parallel to the sea
flax fields threw a drift of otherworldly colour into the greengold day.

On the hill which we spiralled up where the chanting in the conch
of the chapel spilled around us like water we were stilled into some

great silence, even our all-day talking didn't trickle out of it,
as if even the pores of my skin were listening, attentive

like my eyes and ears which were fully alert and still full of the day lilies'
singing as I was learning this Other, this new way of being alive.

You Wrapped in Your Red Coat

We begin by naming. Once
we were two seas and didn't know ourselves;
now by you I know me. This spit of land between
we name 'ours'; it's where the ocean
at last rests.

God is the rain. Is a way of knowing
the whole world. God is the cherry that I lift
from your fingers with my teeth;
the first cherry in the whole
world.

Now God is the ache
in the breastbone that makes us
leave the fireside and wander out
into the wind on the unmarked
ways

where rain rolls in the buttercup fields
and you wrapped in your red coat, shivering.

Later, rain battering
the ox-eye daisies, on our way home
through a dozen shades of blue.
After we've been travelling
so long.

Then this place waiting
like an open hand; fire spitting back
the rain; you pouring tea for me
into the cracked
white mug.

Summer Solstice 2010, Merrivale

[After the horrors of battle] a strange madness came upon Myrddin … Into the forest he went, glad to lie hidden beneath the ash trees. He watched the wild creatures grazing on the pastures of the glades. He made use of the roots of plants and of grasses, of fruit from trees and of the blackberries in the thicket. He became a Man of the Woods, Myrddin Wyllt, as if dedicated to the woods. So for a whole summer he stayed hidden in the woods, discovered by none, forgetful of himself and of his own, lurking like a wild thing.

Geoffrey of Monmouth, *Vita Merlini*, c. 1150

i

in the ruins of the old school house
(four winds, one beech tree
two ragged skewbalds)

nine writers
open the notebook of day

ii

red-sheathed bog cotton
flutters its pennants like snags of cloud
misplaced thoughts
or prayer-flags

iii

lift this granite pebble
from the ochre stream bed
from the water's conversations

the pebble's granite angles
receive and transmit light
resist my palm

iv

the year has come to fruition
what still needs release
before the slide through harvest-time
back to the fallows?

v

after the battles and bloodshed
what remains is peace

the mysteries of love
are stronger than the mysteries
of death

vi

we walk the pairs of stones
in our procession
in a covenant with the past
and with silence

vii

in the 11 stones of the circle
its 4000-year-long discourse
with leaf bird stone wind sky
the day is both clear and opaque

viii

the winds skim our heads
but we've stilled
condensed to light and shadow

we put on the woods of the drovers' track
like a green cloak

ix

Su says
I wear my dad on the inside, his heart

the land listens

x

the pebble is a passing moment
stalled into matter and time
stony bones reassembled
like mine
from atoms
dust of fallen stars

and all of us
spinning in space

xi

the pebble is
my contract
with silence

in the world's hurry
this will endure

Earth Heart Days

for Hanneke

Step out into the field of my heart
wet white buddleia, blue-tit
shaking blades of grass, crazy august rain
and friend with whom I laugh cry dance
whom I love as much as this heart
lets me with its nebulae and galaxies
of nearness and farness

step out into the field of my heart
with its warm blood swarming
its cells in their continual
expansion and contraction
waveparticlewave
made of all there is
xylem and phloem of earth and sky

step into my heart again, dog
newly dead under the apple trees
already going back into all there is
in grace
for nothing stays the same
but this   but this
we know this and everything hurts
and everything is filled with joy
and everything is perfect as it is
rain buddleia blue-tit dog friendship

and oh my friend raise a glass
to the rain and the day with me
to the clouds behind which
all the hearts of stars still burn
raise a glass to these long years of friendship
and promise me that when we come
to die it'll be laughing dancing praying

AIDAN ANDREW DUN

The world is now beginning to hear of Timothy Treadwell, ecowarrior of Long Island, who took off thirteen summers to the wildernesses of Alaska to commune with 'killer' bears.

Through the nineties he became familiar on Canadian channels, cussing wardens and reserve managers who still today exploit the wilderness for tourism and who often have absolutely no kinship with the spirit of grand fearsome mythological animals. Unarmed, Treadwell protected the bears in their threatened habitat.

He defied hunters with their arrogant firepower, ran circles round the authorities, taunting them. He treated them all in the opposite manner to the respectful way he related to his dangerous but lovable friends. Yet Treadwell had another agenda, a mystical shamanic one. He claimed the bears had cured him of heroin and alcohol addiction. He became a media star. Childlike himself in some ways, he worked brilliantly with schoolchildren. Then, in 2003, his life ended, suddenly, tragically. Timothy Treadwell was killed, decapitated, and eaten by an ageing ostracised member of the bear community. (He died a brave man defending a girlfriend who accompanied him, against his will, that last summer.) A generation mourned this strange being.

It then was down to the genius of modern German cinema, Werner Herzog, to construct from hundreds of hours of footage the dramatic image of Treadwell shown to the world in Grizzly Man. *Because, astonishingly, yet logically, Treadwell took cameras instead of weapons when he flew to the wastelands, when he had himself deposited by amphibian aircraft on a remote lake beside what he called the 'Grizzly Maze'. Here, obsessively filming himself up close with the bears, in the style of a truly great communicator, he cavorts and sermonises, cracks jokes rap-style, waxes poetic about wild creatures adored, is over-confident and foolhardy sometimes, loopy too perhaps, but gigantically good-hearted and greatly courageous always.*

Timothy Treadwell charmed a nation till the end. Now, in Herzog's film, in Leonardo DiCaprio's forthcoming movie, and in my poem 'Treadwell', he appears as the most daring of twenty-first-century ecowarriors. His fame is steadily spreading cross-planet. His legacy of guardianship of wildness goes on.

Treadwell

Timothy Treadwell, wildman,
lone soliloquising zoomaniac,
singsong shaman of the labyrinth,
popstar recording his masterpiece.

In a wilderness like a subconscious,
take two for the sake of permanence.
Running in realtime, Timothy smiles,
freestyling in the Canadian tundra.

Hyperborean peninsula landscape,
Tim's flow on-camera, easy, warm.
Solo Treadwell. Transformational
saint with the urge to love beasts.

Wonderfully sane Timothy on earth,
Christopher Robin on strong acid.
Sentry of Eden, serenader of bears:
grizzly-eaten man of the far north.

Metropolitan blond refugee with
drinking problems, drug histories.
(Out comes delivery, transmission.)
In middleground a Kodiak watches

Timothy's back for him, hell-bent,
spitting lyrical hymns on the precipice.
Take it again! Tripod, stand ready
like a tree, guarding life on earth.

Poet of suicidal clips, Tim giggles
as Teddy enjoys a full spinal massage,
nine-foot mother up against a pine tree
tracking mad Treadwell with hairy grin,

The bear-dance of shapeshifting Timothy;
who hibernates shyly, from time to time
confesses himself on celluloid, goes
public, tells of risk, the outside chance.

Here's Tim singing sunshine lullabies
to a Kodiak female lying on her back
nursing at milky boobs her two kids
balanced on the paradise of her belly.

He telepaths friendly playful feelings,
resonates with bears, who initiate this
infiltrator, white man of crazy wisdom
becoming bigger than a whole race.

Here's the free-ranger in tree-posture.
(Live footage; high summer sundown.)
Paradise for T-man: two clear months.
'I tread the great maze of Ursa Major.'

Now Prince Valiant adjusts his fringe,
androgynous samurai cast in a sitcom
with ten-foot actors who dwarf him,
puer aeternus, orphan of Arcturus.

Blood-brother of the subarctic fox,
go well! Walk easily a moonless night,
wise warrior, the new boundaries
between your world and the beast's.

Tin-food; one-man tent: no weapon!
That would be disrespectful to *them*.
He's here as nonviolent video witness,
culture-hero of Vancouver, Toronto.

Miraculously cured junky Treadwell
whole again, ex-dipso, crusading
champion of the new reconciliation
between nature and the bipedal tyrant.

Offering himself as ecstatic intermediary
from the street-wars, handsome Timmy
is rock 'n' roll naturalist, martial artist,
sacrificial patsy, falsetto St Francis.

Here's Tim as rainmaker, threatening
the old meteorological pantheons,
daring a grey sky to show compassion.
(Tears of wonder as demands are met.)

Here's Treadwell as therapist to brown bears:
he lectures, commiserates, romances,
acts as instructor to a combatant
alpha-male savaged in a love-triangle.

See Christ among the dumb animals,
teaching the beasts respect for peace.
(It's Kinski's second coming as Timothy
Treadwell, resurrected from the dead.)

The deep north makes Treadwell a man:
Dexter of the cities, another scumbag,
hits Alaska and the superman emerges,
selfless, ready to die for a greater good.

The Great Bear points to the Pole Star,
the centre, another condition of life,
the lion and the lamb in each other's arms.
Wildman kisses beast full on the lips.

Almost ursanthropy, metamorphosis.
Man into animal; dregs into God.
Timothy reborn as Lady Nature's lover,
conjuror of the forest. Sacre du Printemps.

He pushes a big friend away by the snout.
No pussyfooting round this adversary!
(The past is just a memory of paralysis.)
A rough bark: 'Dude. Get out of my space.'

Here's Timothy T's (twin Tau for crucifixion)
last rant against the keepers of the earth:
nature-boy turns nasty, unacceptable
foaming of the prophet in a cold Eden.

He's here to protect the Honeysuckers
from the man with the firepower, gun-
mad sicko fatso motherfuckers, killing
bearcubs just for kicks in the peninsula.

Only one shortwave call to back out.
But who'll speak for *them?* A carnivore
sleepily inspects the half-naked interloper.
Will His Majesty behave like a gentleman?

Big bad grandpa, cast out of the group,
arthritic, sick, knee-deep in the river,
missing a rightful fish in the waterfall,
eyes young Timothy grumpily, greedily.

Peacemaker. On the last day he'll exit
in front of camera rolling (audio, no
images). Leave that to imagination,
underground Herzog's filmic obsequies.

But no telling like this footage. Fantasy:
Enkidu running with the timber wolves,
fighting Gilgamesh, modern city dweller
whose mind has been chemically sedated.

Thirteen perfect summers running,
transcendental madman, almost in
the arms of the bears he worshipped
with cool evangelistic fascination.

Now he walks up the river to Eden:
two brown giants behind, flanking,
accompany Timothy, escort him into
not-for-the-faint-hearted-country.

Drink, Treadwell, of the wilderness,
that old slow sweet honey of death.
Rest, decapitated hero. Not in vain
your kind, pure fool, comes again.

DIANA DURHAM

Sonnets

Detour

Is that a road to anywhere? The sun's
great gold ball waiting at the end, spilling
gold down its broken asphalt, at the turn
the sign says Detour, where is it going?

This side, the shambolic trees of winter,
tips edged red with fire, penned in like unruly
spectators behind the chain link border
on the other, left over huts, poorly

developed zonings, new office build half planned
these are the strange lands, are they the wastelands
that fall between our seeing? I want to see
the way the sun does, so excitedly

glowing as if this detour, forgotten
scrap of town, led to the door of heaven.

Blake

What bravery, what extremes, completely
to leave the world and etch the real one:
engrave it, ink with rainbow, then copy –
world everlasting, repeatable, done;

and listen only to voices inside
not the outside, political rabble's
rush to the bottom financial scrabble,
take dictation, write songs and hymns, abide

the time when valley's green can meet again
inside our hearts, that realm whose pure exchange
does not pollute; single-handed counter-
balance, counter-culture, who was madder –

poet of fire, brimstone, smoke stacks, vision
of sadness, small cold rooms' introversion.

What Was the Original Wild?

What was the original wild? Was it
wilder than the new? Unkempt waste edges
of the golf course, lost black where the tracks split,
wild west, volcanic, primeval places –

renewing wilderness that we search for,
are you pristine, first, or just unworked yet,
the everywhere emerging dark ore
of newness that only vision can smelt?

Constantly the stream pours, and constantly
we see it, renewable energy
we can never run out of; this light source
of all beginnings, sustainable force

is the first wild, is ours only, untamed,
engendering all we order in its name.

Big Valley, Pennsylvania

an Amish community

the dark green tall waves of the hills, rising
and following the road, their long shoulders
like stilled, slow surf in an ocean moving
to a different time, distant other

time, they rise like giant waves of legend
and the wide open broad-bottomed valley
floats between, carries on a calmer sea
the thoughtful farms, fertile, mulched, well-tended

time after time of choosing this closed world
to catch there something unseen by others
the cloud patterns trailing down the wooded
slopes, long swift scatter of birds on silver

skies, the dark deep intoned presence of soil
the wait of seasons, the rhythm of toil.

Icing

the ice coating
has skimmed the winter grass blue

and the maples' dark wet rust
is fringed mist grey

everywhere a shimmer
of silver, pale grey sheen
of things thinning out

as if the brown, green solid white
January world
is play-acting
its own disappearance

so eyes can see
the invisible nature
that the clear-paned heart
shares

a sea of glass
that in the end
is not anything
but transparency,
a medium for light.

Black River

The river ran black out of the black shade
of arching trees, its dark origins lost
in a depth of woods, its wide flow measured
and unhurried as solemn, marvellous music;

and with it were carried, because it was autumn,
as far as eye could see and further,
gold flecks, gold leaf, gold leaves.
Stately as a great procession

the black river bore them, out of the bronzed
and faded canopy, down into the valley's
tussocked curve, crafted from the season's
careless alchemy, endlessly advancing.

Countless, numberless, they glittered
on the fluid dark, steadily streaming onwards,
more still to fall, and in this way
becoming like the endlessness

of stars moving in the night sky,
broad, glinting swirls of the Milky Way,
bright filaments of light's vast display,
effortlessly stitching everything we see.

KAREN EBERHARDT-SHELTON

I woke in the night and, near-sighted as I am, gazed out the window at the fullest moon imaginable. It was radiant, unwinking, stunning …

Heavenly Moon

This perfectly round tangerine lit from within
pulled me from sleep to stare at my face.
Its serene silence beaming a message:
*Don't close your eyes, come slide through the night
with me as if I was part of your dream*, it whispered
like a voice coming out of my pillow or the glass
in my windows or even the walls of my room;
a grain in the universe magnified to majesty
in the garden of earth's precious atmosphere.

I craned my head upward, half awake,
and there it was patient and watchful,
like God in a hot air balloon herding the stars,
this soothing cool body sliding through heaven
like a round-eyed glowing guardian
of galaxies; or just a bright round mother
gliding calmly over the sleeping lanes and fields
and half the fretful souls on earth,
binding us together in a prayer of passing light.

Five Billion Simultaneous Heart Beats

Calcutta looks like an anthill on the moon.
I fall over myself, watching.
In Varanasi, the scaffolding of the deceased
clogs the river.

Our friends – the French, Brazilians, Ugandans,
the Greeks, one billion Chinese.
India has popped a seam.
She builds that pyramid of bones.

Mexico City sinks beneath the weight of human feet.
Egyptians who inhale Cairo air must lie down.
There is a faint brushing, brushing ...
Like kimonos kneeling on tatami mats,
like bare soles slapping marble at the Taj Mahal.
Like Burmese smearing jungle leaves with sweat.
Like Ethiopians dying thirsty in the dust.

Between stop lights in New York,
cousin-of-lemming crowds are jigging in the streets;
an ambulance is trapped between 59th and Lex.
Infinity expands in L.A.;
in one light year you reach the far side
and are too aged to return.
Of Bangladesh it is better not to speak;
water and bodies hold the earth in place.

And Santa Rosa, California, where too many
new bedrooms are waiting
and maternity wards have waiting lists.

20

Casablanca, Kiev, Sofia, Istanbul, Rome, Karachi, London, Honolulu, Durban, Hong Kong, Bombay, Marseilles, Kuala Lumpur, Peking, Sydney, Buenos Aires, Tel Aviv, Kathmandu, Singapore, Seoul, Port Moresby, Moscow, Rangoon, Havana, Belgrade, Athens, Madrid, Budapest, Montreal, Nairobi, Manila, Kabul, Dakar, Auckland, Berlin, Santo Domingo, Baghdad, Lisbon, Kingston, Djakarta, Belfast, Warsaw, Vienna, Dublin, Palermo, Munich, Chicago, Stockholm, Amsterdam, Santiago, Dallas, Bangkok, Mombassa, Tehran, Bogota, Leningrad, Mecca, Kampuchea, Jerusalem, Colombo, Geneva, Prague, Brussels, Toronto, Dar-es-Salaam, Seattle, Venice, New Delhi, Tokyo, Reykjavik, Paris, Madrid, Angkor Wat, Tenerife, Anchorage, Calcutta, Hobart, San Francisco, Paris, Suva, Lahore, Anchorage … the end of the world, the bottom of the sea breathing with one vast set of lungs, and humans' cities forgetting they don't fit.

The Face of God in the Folded Sheets

What I see in lines and swirls of earth
whole and in parts
translate the hidden panorama
into small breathing hearts
and I am there linking
with cells of who we are.

Do I dumb through a life
of automatic ritual?
I don't know is the question
I always ask.

Where then are we going
what are we touching
in this land of cars and big buildings
selling parts unrelated to who we are?
Who is asking?
The roundabout is clogged
with automatic drivers.

Then I sniff my cat, the old towel
beetroot and butter
the corners of my bathroom;
what lurks where verbs
would love to speak.

Heart then in the hedgerows
music in the stormy wood
a taste of god in folded sheets
my mind a beauty seeking truth.

Lovely golden earring of moon. September like a soothing sofa. The next sofa takes away
the cushions. CAN YOU BE TRULY COSY ON YOUR OWN? I doubt it.

Misplaced Calibrators

Somewhere the mind went missing, then the ear
the mouth, the legs – even the entire family.
Not vanished, just *absent*, tied to an electronic string.

Mum walks the springer spaniels while talking
on her mobile phone;
ladybirds crawl away, bees watch in amazement.

The pub's all a-glitter
machines racheted up – come play!
Be bop, do-lop, rah-rah-rah over frothy rims of beer.

The apples I examined to the core
came from – where was it? Italy, Portugal, Spain? –
somewhere apples have no name or roots
except what Sainsbury's designates.

I reached out – and there was a vast quarry
humming with lorries and broken earth
The red essence pleading for remorse or just
introspection, a repeal of Development.

I look up at that fine sickle of moon
silently laughing, attending, making do
with the aberrant masses it gleams over, asking
what they would do if there was no moon
or sun or seasons ever again –
would they continue their daily shopping
and each night wait for TV to light the room?

Sea-ing into the Haze

Those cliffs are like a dissolving body
washed by space.
The chuckle of water
carrying words from China
announcing its new glut of products.
A panel of light above the horizon
suggests an eye opening to the sea.

This cold day in Maidencombe
whispers deep in its throat:
Oh, watch me. More powerful than you,
but still scarred by what you do to me.

The linked epiphanies of swell and rock,
the breath beneath the tide,
the six ships sitting on a far ripple
as they wait to come inside;
and there, a blackbird confiding from a limb.

Wake up and find the sea
while you still float without regret.
Listen, listen. Watch.
You still have so much to take inside.

God's Underwear

God has been wandering around the village
And across the moors
Lonely in his white boxers, cold and muscular

I heard his two faint cries
In a passing fox and far owl
The only true wild things to visit my dreams

The night air smells like smoked salmon
Except for that crying in the fishy dark
I am alone. I offer God clothes

Hoping he might come near and take them
But only his fox-like shadow sniffs
And those owl eyes never blink

He is everywhere, like spoor
In scented shadow absorbing our conversation
Yet when I touch, the form is empty

Suggesting God doesn't fraternise
That obviously. I must *become* an animal, cast off
And *then* we will be together as a world

ROSE FLINT

Prayer for Always Peace

I ask all the animals to open their mouths
to howl this prayer for peace

I ask all the birds to lift their songs to the winds
and sing this prayer for peace

I ask all the trees and flowers, all that is green growing
to open their hollow throats where the sap runs
to call this prayer for peace

I ask the rocks to dream this prayer for peace

I ask the sand to rearrange its grains
and write this prayer for peace

I ask the ocean wave to shout this prayer for peace
or whisper it on the lonely listening beaches
where the rivers will send it upstream
in the willing breath of fish

I ask the deep wells to give rise to this prayer for peace

I ask the holy hills to toll this prayer for peace

I ask the stars to shine the spelling
of this prayer for peace

and the moon and the sun pause in the sky
as night and day, as right and left, as east and west
as all that is opposite yet may still come into balance
in harmony with this world, and in time

I ask for every candleflame to ignite this prayer for peace
so that this prayer is in the world and of the world
and becomes the world and the world is peace.

Field of Light

If I grieve for the loss of this bright field,
for this small water-vole in the silver river,
for this frail and ancient tree of life, this place
of ordinary light   and if in grieving
know all these will find their deaths – as I too –
in the void that is Her darkness, Her mystery – if
I cherish grief as carefully as I cherish love, then

I can trust to *not-knowing*. I can put my soul
to the work of singing the bones back into the future
of sometime, someplace: honoured, loved, whole –
even changed into beauty beyond all recognition.

Running on Empty

I ran from my Mother before I was born
(and she'd tried so hard, made me of star-ash, clay, rain)
but I raced downtown and went chasing the easy speedy
routes over fields of fuel (feet dirty, heart hungry),
trawling the wide mouth of my Fendi sack for spoils,
discarding and trading: *uranium, copper and cotton,*
bodies and palm oil, sugar, coffee, coal futures, gold –

Someplace I spilled babies, somewhere I drew crowds,
but I rushed on faster, eating and spitting out riches,
winding higher and higher through wasteland and mountain
until I reached the edge and stopped – with nothing before me.

Sirocco and shadow have formed the last of my family:
Grandmother Earth, stick-thin and bony, so fragile, so
easily broken; scorched, hairless, dry breasted, abraded –
Only the two of us matter, only us in existence.

I could leave her. Go on running on empty –
or take off my Prada jacket and wrap it around her,
set tinder to flame in my shoes and sit at her feet, listening
to Wisdom: the First voice of Spirit, breath of the future.

Sedna at Tadusack

Fierce Dark Salt Mother

I dreamed that Sedna stood up out of the ocean
skyscraper high, bright as the sun, glassy
with white sea flowing and falling to dress her
in blue fathoms, green powers and silvers.

She held up her apron of living water
and in it, this spit of land, the long wide river,
the whales that curve through the tide
all lay at peace in their day's work and her love.

Sedna cherishes this rare place where Pattern
is woven by working between light on the waves
and the land, between dark's deep indigo, stars
and whales' cold cycles of song; between peoples.

Sedna, care for us all. Even though we wring the sea
dry with our nets, teach us in time to reweave
the World Pattern, so all oceans, all lands and peoples
may balance together, in the sling of your deep sea love.

Another World Is Possible

Another world is possible.
We can dream it in, with our eyes
open to this Beauty, to all
that Earth gives each of us, each day
those miracles of dark and light –
rainlight, dawn, sun moon snow, stormgrey
and the wide fields of night always
somewhere opening their flower-
stars – this, this! Another world is

possible. With river and bird
sweet and free without fear, without
minds blind to harmony, to how
we can hold. We have been too long
spoiled greedy children of Earth,
life of rocks and creatures
slipping out of our careless hands.
We must stand now and learn to love
as a Mother loves her child, each
cell of her, each grain of her, each
precious heartbeat of her that is
ourselves, our path and our journey
into our dream of future, where
another world is possible
cradling this one in its arms.

DAWN GORMAN

Apple Tree

You gave me an apple tree
that Christmas:
unexpected;
new life
from past love.
I planted it on the lawn
and fussed around it
as if it were newborn,
worrying about
codling moth
and when to prune it
and the high winds
that might lean it
and wincing
when removing
tiny apples
from thin branches
to make the others
grow large and firm.
You gave me an apple tree,
the perfect gift,
spreading today
into the future
like pollen on bees.
You gave me an apple tree

but I maintained my distance
because roots in the earth
are one thing,
but those that delve
skin and flesh
and test
scars and bruises
are quite another.

Tenacity

For those who feel the long, cold winter
has taken it all,
that slivers of ice have sliced
through their world,
that January has,
like an incompetent magician
made friends disappear
from curtained hospital beds
and failed to return them
when the drum roll begins,
and for those who look
at the grey skies of lost jobs,
house fires, accidents, betrayal
and think
'this is insurmountable'
think again.

There is an island
off the coast of Africa –
let us call it, as many do,
'the island of eternal spring' –

where you can crunch across
the black cinders
of a dormant volcano:
a bleak, lunar landscape,
where the hill's contours
are still buried
beneath the giant's dark spew
a hundred years later.
But, but … in that unlikely,
soil-less, grassless,
still-blackened landscape
Canary pine trees have since
grown tall, bold,
pushing through piles
of barren granules,
conjuring woods, birds, insects
from charred, crisp nothing.
Some 98 years, then,
of hard-won effort
but, just when
the island had allowed itself
a small sigh of relief: fire.
A galloping, ravenous inferno
feasting on everything
in its path, reminding
the cinders themselves
of where they'd come from.
Flames swept across
the round belly and
buttocks and thighs
of hillsides,
grabbing the trunks
and branches
of those pioneer trees,
stripping them bare.
When the heat finally died

the world was, once again,
monochromed:
black-barked, limbless pylons
on twice-black ground.
A landscape of defeat?
No, no.
'Defeat' is not a word
in nature's vocabulary.
Just patience. Pause.
Then rain, deluge
and an insistent
irrepressible urge:
Grow. Grow.
Do it, do it, screw it
just do it.
No what-ifs, no regrets,
sorrows, doubts, self-pity.
And then, a tiny speck of green
springs straight from
a charred trunk:
a needle of life reaching
to put a stitch
in thin air.
Then more, more,
bright, unreal,
child's paintbox green
whirls unravelling
into long, fine spikes
sharp with the point of it all,
fluffing out into ruffs,
which spread to catch rain,
channelling water
to new, precious cones
at the centre of a
rediscovered universe.
From a distance, these

phoenix trees
seem to let off their
giddy green fireworks
with a joy we would all do well
to emulate:
the joy of 'grit-your-teeth,
I'm-still-here,
I-can-still-make-a-difference
wipe-that-frown-off-your-face'
survival.

Spring Warriors

Spring is not the time for shrinking violets.
It is a fierce campaign led by snowdrop ice-maidens,
their gutsy umbrellas opened against the odds,
against minus 17 stay-in-bed, why-bother-itis.
'Spring' is a good word for it –
coiled up potential energy,
a launch pad, a drive,
an Alka-Seltzer fizz of irrepressibility,
a push like a mole scrabbling to the surface,
a blind confidence in summer, a future.
The birds join the offensive by February,
and, as if they have swallowed the fizz down whole,
let it rush from their breasts like thrilled battle cries
calling bare branches to arms.
If plants, too, could be heard,
some would already be loud,
the pale yellow primrose yelling beneath the oak trees,
the dangle of dizzy green catkins an exuberant shriek:
we are here, we are here, look at us –
we are on the march,
we are unstoppable.

Natural Order

These hills were too unruly.
We had to stamp
our imprint on them,
pull them into line
with rows of solid houses,
churches, an abbey, a station,
things to steady the seasons,
hold everything together.

The arch of the Palladian bridge locks
trees and bank in a stone frame,
all the edges trimmed.
Walkers lasso flowers and insects
with Latin names;
twitchers tick lists
arranged in alphabetical order.

But it is the spaces we breathe in –
the field where a battle
may or may not have taken place,
the heron which calls to mind
some undefined prehistoric creature,
the swans which may or may not be a pair.
Uncertainty flings things wide open,
lets chance and inspiration flood in.

Holy Well

A stiff, rooked, January morning,
a narrow track,
your sleeves bush-pulled,
layers of frozen footprints.

A sudden clearing.

Two trees giddied with votive ribbons,
shoelaces, bits of plastic bags, and
well-made steps down to a keyhole pool
where the sign sums it up:
The water is no longer safe to drink.

But you dip your hand
under the low, icicled arch
and see the sun catch the water
and watch frozen air move
with a twist of steam.
And you can almost put faith
in a sudden clearing.

Quarry

The white shock of gouged chalk
locks the eye, craters the imagination.
It is more an addition than a removal:
a dazzling, inverted monument
to those who delve and scoop
back to where it all started.

Tracks and ridges emerge in the dust
like the foundations of some ancient
settlement abandoned in snow,
but the site is unhistoried far beyond man –
once, they discovered pliosaur bones;
perhaps, one day, they'll find God.

ALYSON HALLETT

Moon

She is slow as she goes – dragging
her luminous skirts behind a cloud.

    Governess to the weak and the willing
    she scratches the skin
    of her swimmable seas –

mice roar and the sapling shoot
conceives the height of a tree.

    She opens her flowers inside me.

Moon milk instructs the seed to grow,
water to flow, the mind to go
beyond the gate at the end of the lane.

Transparencies

Rocks offer their faces
to the wind and sea.

They want to be eaten, eroded.
Want the inner substance
to be brought to the surface.

One day, these rocks will be sand
and that sand, food for a furnace.

This is how glass is made,
how the densest material
becomes transparent.

It's the same with the darkest
parts of our souls.

The day comes when they want
to offer themselves to the elements,
to the weathers of being human.

I'm talking about breaking things down.
About transformation.

About how things
that are too heavy to carry
can change and lighten.

O Rain

O rain
fast tracked from sky to earth
percussive, rivering, babbling.

O rain
wet world, wet knickers, wet face
water racing wherever it can and will.

O rain
swilling and rinsing dry city streets
tired feet, parched daisies and dandelions.

O rain
eager to meet lost pals, piss cousins
last year's recycled puddle recycled again.

O rain
the sea in me recognises you
as the stranger I once knew.

O rain
remember when we fell down the mountain
and moistened the earth with our dreams?

La, la, la

or

The Singing that Joins Us to This Rock

Stones are singing today.
Songs so complex and legend
only a dream dreamed in carbon dark
can hear them. I lie down,
shut out the crying gulls
and listen as whales are said to listen,
with my whole body – bones, blood, lungs
and skin attuned to the frequencies
of Earth. Deep in the triune brain,
in the maze of pre-human pathways,
a lizard appears. It knows how to hear
and how to sing along, *la, la, la,* then
oooo, aaaa, eeee – yes,
there is still a wilderness within,
still nature in this compound of skin:
the granite songs, the slate songs,
Precambrian limestone songs – yes,
there is still this desire to join in.

What We Do When We Stop Talking

No one teaches us how
to be born
    and no one's going to teach us
        how to die.

   The answers are already
     inside us
        and all we need to do is listen.

So what if we're scared?

               So what if we don't know
          what we're doing?

       You think the rocks are certain?
Look at them, they're full of faults.

      You think that tree's got it all mapped out?
Please.
        It's bending under the weight
of the wind and twisting back on itself
      to find the light.

Why do you think the sea practices so much?
     Wave after wave after wave –

  I tell you, we need to stop all this talking
      and listen. Yes I tell myself, I need to
stop all this talking and listen.

Suddenly Everything

I've been watching clouds.
Sunday clouds above an estuary
stung with jet skis and sailing boats
with junk red sails. The speed
of them, the endless bleed of one
into the other.

'I never paid any attention
to clouds before,' the dying man says.

His fault then, that I'm lying here like this
looking at clouds as if they were the most
important things.

The idea behind the atmosphere.
The very things that guarantee life
on this tumbling bauble of rock.

Clouds bloom and dissolve
as the green hand of the wind
gardens their moist, white bodies
from one fantastic flower into the next.

No holding on up there.

The dying man is called Wolfgang.
'Every cloud outside my window,
every flower in the vase,
suddenly everything matters,' he says.

JEREMY HOOKER

To the Unknown Labourer

No monument
For time to smear;
No statue
That a man conceives
To trap himself in stone.

Only earth
Where a night's rain
Washed out his prints;
Chalk where his life
Was moulded;
Fields like hands after work,
Rough palms spread.

Nobbut Dick Jefferies

(*'See'd ye out on the downs?'*
'Nobbut Dick Jefferies moonin' about.')

No one but him
Mooning in a backwater
Of the nineteenth century
We've walked apart from the houses
And here, on the edge
Of a common under pines,
Light in every facet
Dances round his words

Such tenderness
Is unbearable
The point of a grassblade
On the eyeball

Even from the flowerhead
Of a slender foxtail, a branch
Grows over the earth's side
And he has stopped where it bends
Trying the body's weight
Against the bough's strength

The knowledge
Will not disclose itself,
Nor the world make something
Of him, though the extremity
Starts from its roots.

Landscape of the Daylight Moon

I first saw it inland.
Suddenly, round white sides
Rose through the thin grass
And for an instant, in the heat,
It was dazzling; but afterwards
I thought mainly of darkness,
Imagining the relics of an original
Sea under the chalk, with fishes
Beneath the fields. Later,
Everywhere upon its surface
I saw the life of the dead;
Circle within circle of earthen
Shells, and in retraced curves
Like finger marks in pale sand,
The print of a primeval lover.
Once, climbing a dusty track,
I found a sunshaped urchin,
With the sun's rays, white
With the dusts of the moon.
Fetish, flesh become stone,
I keep it near me. It is
A mouth on darkness, the one
Inexhaustible source of re-creation.

Walking all day in the Forest

Walking all day in the Forest, I saw again how impossible it would be to convey a true impression of the ancient woods of oak and beech without showing that they are movements of light and shadow and air as much as countless tree-shapes, or rather that the natural 'pattern' continually changing around one comes from the interaction of forces and things which together make a world of the most delicate and subtle movements. And strong, deep-rooted forms. And this is only to sketch the surface, without regard to the interdependence of growth and decay, or of the many forms of life each with its own world in the world that human senses perceive; as for example insects under a scale of bark, a grey squirrel leaping from tree to tree, a woodpecker crossing a glade.

Cyane

Finally a body that is water's own.

So at times words seem to come to me,
as though I could speak,
or as I remember speaking in another life.

I pool to a glassy stillness.
I move slowly, mirroring
shapes & colours of leaves;
housefronts, walls; a face;
the world entranced
gazing at the world.

Or quick, a stream
of silver – only
what I know is imageless,
except once, in another life …

My moods are stagnant,
turbulent. I circle circle circle,
or stand motionless, or pour out,
falling, scattering,
coming together with the smoothness
of a dolphin's back, an icy glide.

What was I before I was finally this?
Sometimes I dream that on my surface
I form a human face,
and look out at another,
red and glistening, a man's,
and arms, in which he grasps a woman,
binds her to him, drags her down.

And it shakes then: earth quakes,
and springs apart – they are gone.

And I shake, the being that I was –
                    skin blood bones
unbinding, flying into drops,
flowing with a constant tremor,
plunging down, shattering,
shaking out long and smooth,
always broken, always whole.

And over I go and over,
and under, and round and round.

But what is that but a dream
that I was human once,
who am pure spirit,
not bodied, not bodiless,
but water in water, quick
with a life beyond all words.

Silence, then; or a voice
that is the sound of water running,
in which, if they listen,
any one may hear a tale
of terror at the roots of things:

a tale that I tremble to tell,
half remembering, or inventing,
but as if, once, it were my own.

ADAM HOROVITZ

Second Coming

brought down to earth
with needless force

burnt alive
as a matter of course

the Second Coming
has a bitter taste

an acid fistful
in the face

Wile E. Coyote Pauses for Thought

All these unthinking technocratic years
shooting myself from giant rubber bands
and pawing vitamins
– the kind that build your limbs
into flexible hillsides –
down my ravenous throat
and here I still am,

a blurring swarm of legs
scrabbling at molecules of air,
waiting for the river-rush of sun-red stone.

Nature has its favourite ways of saying *No*:
earthquake, tsunami, volcano.
The acme of *That's all folks!*
But I've encountered subtler signs;
now I am certain
that the cliff face, not the bird,
opens up the tunnels
I can't run through,
that boulders shift and twitch into my way
as the desert dreams of my defeat.

There is a lesson to be learned,
which does not fit onto the tiny signs
I use to whisper my goodbyes
before becoming yet another
distant puff of canyon smoke.
I must remember that I am a machine,
the pinnacle of pursuit,
must temper my reliance on things other than myself.
No more exploding birdseed, no more backfiring guns.
I must become what I pursue.

This time as I fall I'll yell *Meep Meep*.

The Memory of Water

Do you remember the rain?
No? It was life to us in the cold
days of upheaval, before the fall;
it was mouse patterings on a ceiling of leaves,
a sweet dishevelling
carrying the scent of change.
Like the swallows it came, back
and back again to the places it remembered.

This dust-wheel plain was forest once.
Deep underneath, where nuts and seeds snuggle in,
their ability to grow suspended by the drought,
the memory of water echoes
in empty caverns that were lakes,
shivers in parched fibres, patient as a spider.

Sometimes the rain came down
in a ritual showering, a breathy song of cloud.
Or, in the boomy slate-grey mornings
it was the rush of trains.
We marked the days with it, the seasons
as it balanced on the edge of the horizon
like a scavenging gull.
We were never sure whether we wanted it
to break on our heads like dark, ripe apples
although we loved it when it came.

But the rain that clung like silk,
that slithered in through clothes
to the moist valleys of the flesh,
that is the rain I remember.
The rain that sweetened the breath of gardens,

that clung to your breast like a kiss.
That is the rain I will take with me to my dying.
Let me show you, with my lips,
exactly how it felt.

Seeding

i

They seat me at the mouth
of a bunker of sun-black rocks,
cross-legged and rigid.
The air is thin as watered whisky,
potent as opium.
It scalds my blood, scolds it to silence,
carries the voices of crows,
raised in throaty celebration
– a carrion song reserved for rotting sheep –
across the mountain.
The sun hauls its blazing bones
behind a jaw of rock.
A purple bruise of heather
on the mountain
yammers farewell.
A soft comb of rain
flattens my hair.
I can feel the crows
squeezing sheep's eyes
in their beaks like seeds.

ii

I have been here for weeks,
or maybe months. I cannot tell.
My flesh has adapted, is akin to stone.
Each outward breath
spawns the seeds of clouds.
I am crumbling into myself,
overwriting the past as I watch
weather-beaten, tenacious shrubs
cling to a storm-wrecked raft of granite
in a wine-dark heather sea.
At best, home is unwieldy memory,
at worst, hallucination.
Children, cats and lovers dance,
hazy in the sunlight, into oblivion.
Only the mountain seems real.

iii

The crows tell me bells toll
for the end of my penance
in a tower beneath the sea.
In the flat, forgotten fields of memory
I hear them. They buzz
like a canker full of flies.
All that I knew is gone. The crows
sharpen their beaks on my calves,
peck beetles from the moss in my groin.

CHARLOTTE HUSSEY

Cailleach

She is the blue heron fishing the bleak
pools. Alone, standing for hours
on one clawed foot, she persists,
rooted beside the shrubby willow.

She is the gull with her raucous cries,
cleaning her catch, a dripping eel
gulped down on the railed
bridge crossing the tidal creek.

She is the one called daughter of the little sun,
gliding over the November seas,
like the whirlwinds she always precedes,
ones that can never catch her.

On the slippery rocks beside the whirlpool,
she leans her blue-black face
over what boils like one of her pots,
washing her shawls, washing her shawls

to a whiteness she lays out over the earth,
over the mountains, the hillocks
that once fell like boulders from her apron,
as she waded across the raw bay.

Her crooked hands are reaching over its waters.
Her one good eye, set under a grey brow,
looks twenty miles out to sea
for the oncoming armada. She will sink it.

With her scolding flock, she raises sharp,
piping winds against war lords,
against the cruel. She saves those who are weak
and poor, all the lonely old ones.

Ndixito: From the Life of Maria Sabina

*'Ndixito' in Mazatec means 'Little-Ones-that-Spring-Forth' and refers to the mush-
rooms that the Mexican Curandara Maria Sabina used to heal people; her first miracle
was her own sister.*

1 Bloom

We pop up in the rainy season
in highland pastures, on steep slopes
where the earth is red and alive;
a fist full of thunder, we erupt

out of dung heaps, sugar cane
husks, out of rotten tree trunks
where we perch, pajaritos, little birds,
out of a misty hillock, a landslide.

2 Hunger

We find Maria in a green-black wood.
Cold and starved, she tends
six white chickens scratching,
scratching in the rain-drizzled dirt.

Ravenous she tears us up,
this Wise One, still a child:
'If I eat you, you and you,
you'll make me sing beautifully.'

3 Healer

Her sister, no adult can cure;
Maria Sabina remembers us, gives three of us
to Maria Ana, eats many herself –
soil clinging to our bitter roots.

Pressing pain from her sister's hips,
she sings what we tell her – of the morning star,
the earth, its plants and humming birds –
takes up her staff of sap and dew.

4 Clowns

We spring up. Nobody plants us.
We spring up by ourselves, the flesh,
the voice of Gods some say. We say
little clowns wearing our copper caps.

Tear and eat us up. But if you
drop a piece, one of us will ask,
while working: 'Where are my feet?
Why didn't you eat all of me?'

5 Table

We give the Wise One visions:
a troupe of jugglers and tumblers,
little duendes squatting in the dust,
we dress up as town officials.

Six or seven magistrates seated at table,
we rustle through piles of papers,
table solemn as the Last Supper,
bearing all the things of the world.

6 Book

One of us, bald-headed Sasa,
like a sweet, commanding father,
calls forth our book of wisdom,
pulsating threads of light,

twisting up from the ground. Our book,
its leafy pages bound in white bark,
grows to the size of a snake, a woman,
a white tree, this Book of the Earth.

7 Words

She lovingly caresses our book,
hands passing right through it,
each syllable, each jot of light
swelling up from the warm dark.

Curved lines, triangles, jagged
shapes, we cone-heads, disguised
as little geometric beings,
hop giggling across its pages.

8 Acrobat

Then Durrembe, our finest tumbler,
comes falling like a thunder bolt,
a luminous, blinding object,
head-first through a hole in her hut.

Its blue-green strands of light
branch upwards into a black sky,
a dewy bush covered with
every imaginable flower.

9 Fiesta

Doffing our caps to please the crowd,
we dance on thin, bare legs.
Plucking violins, thrumming our guitarrón,
we make her body hum and twirl.

Small brown feet appear, disappear
under the hem of her whirling skirt –
Dew Woman, Tree Woman,
Great Lord Clown Woman.

from Small Catastrophes: After Reading
Marko Pogačnik

The language of direct physical experience, conveyed through natural catastrophes, remains the main recourse open to elemental beings trying to warn us against the abyss into which we are about to plunge.

Marko Pogačnik

Plane Tree

In the clangour of cement mixers and trucks
paving over soft, sandy paths in the park,
a little urban planner, well-meaning fixer-upper,
comes toting his clipboard and tape measure.

Rattling out his flaccid tool to their ruckus,
he pulls and plies it along my most magnificent branch.
Sticking out mid-trunk, lank and uncharted,
my limb points towards a grassy lane, a ruined palace.

Like no other branch, knobby as an old wrist
kissed by a wood wife, it twists into space, stretching out eight metres,
then spikes straight up: connector, conductor,
divining for power, directing it heavenwards.

'Irregular' is the one word the little man scribbles
on his blue-lined pad, on his flipping clipboard.
Belching gases, the revving chainsaw in his puny hands
bites into my branch, vying for my power.

It is like cutting off the climax of a symphony –
Beethoven the village band strained over
under my shade. Tête-à-tête, the town folk listened,
laid out on the grass, until I made Hades rumble,

clouds heave and foam through molten sky.
It is like no baton to conduct *The Pastoral*,
no wand to conjure a thunderhead, no hand
to compose an untidy billet-doux.

He strikes away my most intrepid part,
leaving a fresh wound, tingling with phantom pains.
Fitfully, they shoot into the air, spilling darkness
onto the hardened path his men pave overtop my roots.

Elementals

Our beaks black as a vulture's,
our legs insect-thin,

we scuttle about on this branch.
No one considers us.

No one even sees us sitting here.
Out of this lack, we band together

to push the sharp sheers
back into the meddling hand

that nips away at our branch.
We push hard. She screams,

teetering on her ladder, as if
bitten by an adder's tongue.

Blood pours down,
red as pared fruit skin,

mixed with mud beside
the torn off work glove.

This is our voice, the only one
you'll listen to.

Undines

A rain of bulldozed gravel and dirt
buries the little river we've guarded,
are tied to beyond human memory. Its waters
strung our beads with a thousand bubbles,
laved our arms as we gathered willows,
concealed our songs in the blackbird's cry,
in the reedy hum of dragonfly wings.
Passerby, you are more solid, more transitory.

Now we wander farmers' fields,
fingering damp spots, fretting over
muddy places near the culverts
our river was forced into. Metal haters,
posing as a thistle bush, or briars,
we'll snag your pant legs. Passerby,
in your pale, weedy garments,
can't you see us churning the air
as if it were water into an addled haze?

IRINA KUZMINSKY

This age of darkness …

This age of darkness
Age of toil and strife
Of services unrendered
and of truth denied
Age of destruction
cataclysms and wars
Age of great hunger
and of hate which gnaws
Age when we fear
to welcome in our sun
Age when air chokes
and rivers cease to run
Age when trees die
denuded of green life
Age when food poisons
and the soil deals death to life
Age of confusion
Age of misused sound
Dissonant age
which now breaks up our Ground

I'll praise this age
For in the midst of suffering and strife
hearing earth groaning
with her children lost to life

Into the clefts of shifting poles and plates
Into the birthing chairs of tidal waves
Into the crystals' spasms and despite
all we can do
She comes – to turn our dying agony
to rainbow hue
Telluric
and with birth convulsed –

This very age
I'll praise
and praise again
For in this age did goddesses
again descend
and walk the earth.

from Quills

Take this pen
Pagan
Take this pen
Inscribe
On your body
I will not harm
This earth.

A Sequence of Embraces

Consider it my gift to you
Life's gift of air …

I have spoken to the birds of Paradise
Bright-coloured
Why go there to seek the houri?
She walks beside you on the sacred earth

*

I am air
I am the wind's embrace
Warm breeze caressing skin
Zephyrs ruffling hair
Cold gusts sharpening minds
Storm winds to ride to your destiny
And whirlwinds to clear out your house –

May the winds come to you
From the North, East, West, South
Choose the wind your life needs
In your seasons of need
My embrace
The embrace of the wind

*

Not my embrace – but fire
Not my waves – but water
Not my touch – but air
That you may know the sacredness of earth

66

*

Embrace me and embrace soul
Lips to lips
Eyes to eyes
Awakening me – you
Awaken

*

I embrace and assert what I am
Serving you serve my essence
Comingle with me and awaken into emptiness
Penetrate me and know your own depths

For I am She who flows
    She who changes
I am She who awakens
Desire – your desire for your
Life

from Australian Stories

How do you fix a broken land?
Insulated in suburbia with prepacked vegetables and meats
With plumbing, gas pipes, wires
With laden supermarket shelves which mock our choices
With choice eroded as we run from freedom
– any compulsion will do –
Enclosed backyard and front
We pace our lawns escaping knowledge –
  We've never known our land
Small wonder we have an identity crisis
No branches without roots
No nation without a land
But we – the uprooted –
Uproot all our trees – family and other –
Scarce bothering to ask
How shall we fix it, our broken land?

KEVAN MANWARING

Breaking Light

for Jenni

i

It is late. It is early.

3 a.m. Too awake to sleep.
Too tired not to.
Feeling the house breathe around me,
its unfamiliar night sounds, a
strange landing.
The pores of my skin
are a million unblinking eyes.
You have set me off
like a spinning top.
Made my head explode with light.

As you lie next to me,
I listen to the white noise
of rain on your attic windows,
whispers in the static.

Even in the city I feel Her near.

Lady Autumn,
I can hear you
washing your long russet hair,
a weeping willow sifting the wind.
The rivulets reveal its lustre,
like a wave-wet pebble on the beach –
your colours unveiled, a whole paintbox.

Everything becomes more beautiful
the more it lets go –
the more it releases its inner life.
The promise of frost brings
the spectrum to the surface –
the colours the light let go of.
We see what isn't absorbed.
A leaf, in Spring, not-green, becomes
in Autumn, not-red.

What the world sees is
what we cannot contain inside us; it
spills out –
breaking light,
the way love splits us open.

ii

It is late. It is early.

Lady Autumn is walking
with sloe-eyed grace
through our lives once again;
rose-hipped, withy-limbed,
bejewelled with blackberries like
tiny bunches of grapes,
ready to burst on your tongue,

lips, fingertips,
stained with juice;
rowan berries, hard as nipples;
elder berries glisten like spider eyes,
from boughs of yellow flames,
watching.

The forest floor
where we made love
sanctified by
your blood, my seed,
mingling with the soil.
Its rich earth of
fertile death
scattered with ash keys, acorns,
fur-flowered beechmast,
horse chestnuts, hard and smooth
in their spiky jackets
(like antiques packed in a sea mine),
the milky bullets of cobs,
walnuts ransacked by Ratatosk
buried in forgotten cists,
fungi erupting from another world,
like fish gasping for breath,
gills gaping.

I graze lazily through your edible forest —
pore my hot breath into your jew's ear,
rifle your king alfred's cakes
and penny buns,
devour your chicken-in-the-woods.

I trace the lace of your mycelia,
the wood's lingerie. I yield
to your moreish morel,
drink champagne from your chanterelle.

You lick my slippery jack,
make my puff balls
explode.

Feral cry in the thicket,
the grunt of wild boar
snuffling out truffles,
the sow's ear of his mate.
A roe deer freezes, wet nostrils twitch,
a flank shivers,
and it leaps into the wood's legend.

The sunlight snags
on the canopy's lattice,
the chlorophyll circuit-board
of a crimson leaf,
the abacus of dew
on a cobweb.

Nature's astonishing
attention to detail
insisting
we notice.

Like an act of love.

I stroke your face
with a tuft of old man's beard,
circumnavigate you with a feather,
all your inlets and promontories.

We cast a limpet shell
on the river
laden with our dreams
and laugh as it sinks.

iii

It is late. It is early.

Lady Autumn
teaches us
the art of letting go,
as she performs her annual yard sale,
de-cluttering with a tut, a smile,
a shake of the head,
tidying away the toys of summer.

She sings as she sweeps –
her long skirts
layered with a patchwork of leaves,
gathering up all that we don't need
in her wake.

Busily she insists
we put our house in order
before the harsher times ahead.
Her winter sister is not so sentimental
when she brings her black bag,
as bottomless as a December night.

Despite all we have done,
the gifts we have squandered,
her treasures plundered,
still the Earth
is beautiful.
Still the Earth will forgive us.
Her compassion is endless,
and we will weep at her feet
before this is played out.

But first, a favourite vinyl crackles
to the centre.
The needle gathers dust.
With a melancholy pang
Lady Autumn revisits her old haunts,
her maiden places,
savouring the memory one last time
before letting it fade.

She presses the best
into the palimpsest of the past,
a bonfire for the rest.
Smoke curlews from the piles of leaves,
gathered into golden dragon hoards,
to be kicked –
and, for a moment,
we are as rich as bank robbers,
the folding gold falling around us.

iv

It is late. It is early.

We finally met
at Lammas –
when summer first seems to sense
its own mortality.
Ours is a late summer love.
Not the foolishness of Spring,
swept along by giddy lusts,
the chancy intoxication of the May,
nor the apparent glory of June,
when midsummer dazzles us
with its gaudy enchantment,

but a love of long shadows,
of languid contentment.

Ripening to prime –
we are ready for love's press.
It insists we offer all.
What can be gained from
withholding the tiniest drop?
Pulp and pith and pip,
let the cloth of truth,
contain our allness.

Gladly we bring our bounty to share
to the harvest supper of the heart.

Arriving in splendour,
wearing our autumn like a crown,
we greet each other
at the end of a long road,
our harlequin robes
stretching behind us.

Stopping to let the sunset slip
like a mug of copper hops
down a thirsty throat
over the blue tapestry of hills
pegged to the sky by trees,
we give thanks for the abundance,
the riches of the year,
strewn before us
with such wild abandon.

Yet the thrift of Mother Earth
means nothing
is wasted.

All the ungathered,
unreachable treasure
that falls on the ground,
unpicked, to rot,
becomes the mulch
from which the future grows.

v

It is late. It is early.

And the world is turning beneath us,
so let us hold onto one another,
for where we go to sleep
is not the same place we wake up.
Everything shifts – the Earth
tilts;
we have only our the axis of our love
to stop us from spinning off into space.

You anchor me
with your eyes,
a touch, a word,
breathed in the night,
a smile at break of day.

We contain each other with such
lightness,
allowing our spaces to dance
against one another.
To make a third shape between.

I inhale you. You exhale me.

I slip into bed, blindly, seeing by heat,
and let the warmth you have left
envelop me.

Our souls fit together,
like our bodies do.

As though,
way back when
before the beginning,
we had been wrought as one,
then, broken apart –
to be finally,
blissfully –
joined once more.

The same light
shining through us both.

Love,
the home where we belong –
the door with our names on –
waiting for us to arrive.

PAUL MATTHEWS

To the Lady

Here I am. There
is the grass outside
and the wide sky;

and you are involved somehow.

It's not a vision I ask for.
Something simpler. Some apprehension
of your glance within this green.

You are a woman certainly. I've seen
where you would have been
if I'd looked a moment sooner.

Lady without footprint.

The slight lean of your head
coincides
with how a bough bends
and makes it girlish.

How you laugh the light.

But sometimes I have found you
in the night side of a leaf –
a grief without eyelids.

Lady I would name you in grass and flower
and speak no word about the spirit.

A Green Theology

Leaves catching light
are the true scriptures

I'm freed then
from the need
to describe them

They describe themselves

They are their own
green messages

It is a book
which the wind is turning

Searching a word

Where each man
reads of himself

Reads into it   theologies
of thrush and sparrow

But the tree itself
seems occupied
with a more urgent matter

Look   how it writhes here

This speech turns
always upon itself

Revealed   and veiled again

Where each man reads
(freed from the need to)
a green theology
which the wind is turning

Carrying Language into a Wood

Aspen is the noisiest tree. It flares
above the quietness of the wood.

*

The bluebells are over. We six
are the only things not green.

*

Loud flowers we are.
Surely we do intrude
with our brash language.

*

Who tore
off the blackbird's wing?
It has one white feather.
We hurry too fast
past all the messages.

*

No one really enters a wood
unless they are prepared
to give up their language.

*

Be like a tree, Michael.
Logs under the saw
scream in pain.

*

Paula is the very last bluebell
deepening to purple.

*

When language falls away
we see that each leaf
bears a name upon it.

*

This paper was a tree once.
If I dropped it in the wood
it would not be litter.

*

Generations of leaves litter the wood.
Our names enter the dark ground.
I love these six people.

*

We have found our initials carved.
Oh this is the best
corner of the world, Michael.

JEHANNE MEHTA

Beltane in England

Oh, this festival of green,
rolling in torrents over the trees,
in the subtlest shades of surprise,
unfurling a boundless fertility:
saplings sprouting in bundles
from a smile wide as the woods,
dimpled with stitchwort and violets.

And we are expecting some
vast desert doom,
where our waste devours the wild
as we go down as into quicksand
with a last rictus of despair.

But She has other plans:
ivy, beech and birch leaves,
shaking out like handkerchieves
from her fat pockets;
leaf casings, rosy as lips,
littering the lanes,
and everywhere, She is agog
for love.

In the old cemetery even the graves
are beds of tufted grass,
inviting unheard of, secret conceptions.

Did you notice the daisies
eyeing you with sun-sharp intensity?

You could not slip out of this game,
even if you wanted to:
the bluebells are longing to explore
your toes,
and the footways are only
a temporary diversion,
surfaces to be reclaimed
by your feet,
in the wink of a green eye.

And the honey bees did not go far,
still weaving their rapid lemniscatory pollen dances,
behind the knotted veils,
waiting for our love-call
back to the hives.

A child in pink tights clambers onto a wall
and jumps.
Who knows where she will land,
wild clematis in her hair,
her core curriculum coiling green
from her schoolbag,
in long tendrils of exuberant vegetation?

And we are expecting some
vast and desert doom,
where our waste devours the wild
and we go down as into quicksand
with a last rictus of agony.

But oh, this festival of green,
riotous, rejoicing.

And are we now too old for love,
our loving days over?

Nothing Now Common

Heat, honeysuckle, pink poppy heads,
city-suited magpies, strutting under limes …

This morning the pear tree was sounding with bee song,
continual soft intoning, relieving the vortical pull on the spine,
the shattered orientation, unsettling leakage of time.

This is no common spring,
nothing now common,
a reaching through of paradise:

hedges going down under blizzards of blossom,
blackthorn, thornless in its Eden white,
cowslip keys releasing the meadows
and blue, full-blown, fervent,
a blue aflame from beyond itself,
under the leaning beeches.

The unbearable sweetness of flowers
tilts the heart out of its easy axis,
tearing us open, like love.

Beneath our closed faces something unknown turns.
Can we live with this heaving and churning
in the fertile ground,
upsetting certainties, unsettling our roots?

She is taking nothing lying down now.
She is about her rebirth, emerging in the vertical plane …
She is awake, here …

inside us.

Yew Pollen

To regrow while you die is a hardy thing
to rejoice in the stirring bud, while giving in
to dissolving bonds, decaying paradigm,
the split and buckling bark of linear time.

In the needle dusk of yew small purses cling,
thick under every twig, gold stocks that could
replenish every heart, balance out the appalling
crumbling of the world. Down flies a bird.

Flit of feather, dipping to a branch and there …
bright puffs of pollen, dusty, shimmering,
dance into the wind, dispersing everywhere.

And look: here at this difficult door of spring,
that fullness of life which was close, shut out of the air,
is coming again in clouds, at touch of wing.

Albion?

This model now, maquette of a masterpiece,
is bent out of alignment along the vertical axis,
the clay cracked, dry, crumbling.
It no longer serves.

Take a new baseboard,
take netting, pliers and strong wire
and build her anew;
but this time, around the armature, not clay,
this time build her, like Blodeuwedd, out of flowers,
bluebells, crosswort, lady's smock
and the wild white cherry;
and set a bee house for her heart,
alive with summer harmonies.
She would be a passion of pollination.

You would sense her sweetness
long before you saw her,
her eyes awake,
alight with recognition,
and love would flow like honey
out of her palms.

Hymn to the Earth

She is lovely in the springtime in her dress of gold and purple;
She is lovely in the summer in her robe of living green;
Lovely in the autumn all clothed in flame and yellow;
Lovely in the winter in her gown of mist and rain.

She is lovely where your feet have trod and left a winding pathway,
Lovely where the deer rests in the warmth of evening sun,
Lovely where the buzzard soars on the west wind from the ocean,
Where the trees talk a green language and the restless squirrels run.

She is lovely where the silver brook sings its endless melodies,
Lovely where your hand has shaped the landscape to your will,
Lovely where the ploughman cleaves her depths to plant the harvest,
And when her fields are cold and bare, then she is lovely still.

In rocks and soil she is alive, alert and always listening;
In beech and ash and sycamore she is watching and awake.
You can sense her body tremble as your heart is slowly opening,
You can feel her move towards you, as you begin to speak.

All down the twisting centuries she has waited for this moment,
For your heart to sing with her heart and dance to the same beat.
In the woods and hills a new earth stirs beneath her secret portals.
A world which only you and she together can create.

MARGIE McCALLUM

Pukerua Bay

I sit astride a huge driftwood log
and look out into the sea.
As far as I can see
the shining waves dance and roll,
rise and tumble, swell and break
in a glorious race
to bring their gifts to me.
Finally they reach the shore,
their elbowing and mock competition over.
One by one, they roll at my feet:
strength
guidance
clarity of purpose
courage
wisdom.
Every helping spirit I could ever need
comes to me, presents its gifts
and disappears again into the whole.

What did you do when you knew the Earth was unravelling?

on listening to Drew Dellinger

What did I do when I knew the Earth was unravelling?

I chose consciously to reduce my impact on her delicate web of interconnectedness, and in my unconscious times doubtless added to her pain.

What did I do when I knew the Earth was unravelling?

I chose work that helped hold back the racing tide of destruction, and allowed my awareness of my children's children's children to enter every level of my thought and action.

What did I do when I knew the Earth was unravelling?

I chose to live from my heart, to love all of it: the trees bursting with life and the weeping, burning tracts of rainforest; the birds that sing in the morning and their brothers and sisters who sing no more; the folks who work to stop the overturning and the folks who hasten its progress.

What did I do when I knew the Earth was unravelling?

I chose to live from a place of joy, to know that resurrection follows crucifixion, that life is not always as it seems, that in the big scheme life is abundant beyond measure.

What did I do when I knew that the Earth was unravelling?

I chose peace as my companion as I walked the sometimes scary
road. I donned her cloak, not against knowing Earth's suffering but
as protection against my own undoing, for what use is an unravelled me?

What did I do when I knew the Earth was unravelling?

Above all I chose to live awake to my true nature, which is the same
as the true nature of all humanity and every life form. I chose to
surrender to the ultimate oneness and beauty of it all.

I chose.

Chalice Well Garden, 2 a.m.

The water, the moon and I are well awake,
alone in almost silence.

The white of Beltane flowering
and a coverlet of cloud
light up the paths, the well,
the ever-flowing Lion's Head.

I ask the Scorpio moon to end in me
whatever keeps me from the Oneness.

The Healing Pool is sombre
and in my mind I walk her waters
re-affirming my entreaty
to the fullness of the moon.

Let no bright colours interrupt the month of May

Let no bright colours interrupt the month of May;
she is the bride preparing for her wedding;
hawthorn and cow parsley,
white satin dress and swathes of tulle.

White she emerges
shy, pure and joyful;
white from the springing green
of new life, new love.

She gathers soft posies –
forget-me-nots and bluebells,
a past to carry colour to her future –
and sun-faced daisies to bedeck her hair.

What lies in mid-summer?
Abundance and brightness,
red and orange of passion and defiance,
purples and blues, royal hues.

But let not bright colours interrupt the month of May.
Gently the bride comes;
beautiful, soft and white.

On Reading Rilke's Letters to a Young Poet

When something rises in me
asking for expression beyond the thinking of it;
when some layer of self is nudged and softened;
may I give it no more trouble than the earth
gives the shoot when it wants to come;
may I allow the deep ground of me to break open,
the sap to rise, the bursting forth
to hold whatever newness seeks a handmaiden;
may it come forth untampered with and wild.

Somerleaze Farm Retreat

What is this time, this place
that found me, merciless in its requirement
to hold a plan of things that stands before me
half unknown and yet in essence traceable
through months of shifting sand beneath my feet?

Set upon this island, not without company
yet apart, remote, an effortsome ride
for me and them; outer work dwindling
while inner work comes, shouting
in the gentlest of ways,
Do not let this retreat time slip you by.
Call in its quiet beauty, slow river,
banks of ransoms, tree-wind, bird-tune;

accept its gift of time, space, solitude
and hungry days.

Do not resist the empty nights
wakeful for reasons you do not need to know.
Throw yourself upon its strangeness;
let both heart and mouth say No
to interferences from any sphere.

A few months; a few months –
such quick passing will ask you
frightening soon
did you draw deep, lay bare,
surrender to the coming?

Will you speed your days
as fast flows the middle river,
murky and eddying,
or will the clear shallows,
still and reflective,
be your remembrance?

GABRIEL BRADFORD MILLAR

The Fere

(O.E. – mate, companion)
after 'Ballad of the Goodly Fere' by Ezra Pound

Famed be   Your feorhus
for its   fairness,
for its   fine perfection.
If You stand   six feet
in sandals,   so tall
may we   one day stand.
When we have   worked and won,
when we   by white magic
turn sword   to psaltery,
when we   by white will-might
shift slaughter   to song.

Am I Ready?

Am I ready
to greet the breathing earth?
She's ready,
past ready.

How shall I reply
to the passionate planet –
vermillion in the west
and the hill brooding indigo?

Green ground in the morning,
generous and strong,
rosebay willow herb,
fat apples and mallow?

I am plagued by the gravity
of this sacred charge
to praise her,
to state her case.

Pitchcombe

October has started in the village,
stretching spur fingers into the hedgerows.
Crisp at the tip they are, like a nurse's,
causing the birds to think of softer seasons
or the journey south.

Not yet the snow that cripples every enterprise
but the tracking of hares through the upland wood,
though the air comes like a knife
into our cotton clothes.

The house that was a mill, and the lily pond
have sat through four centuries of seasons,
mellow and marking time, while reports came
from the volatile capitals that nothing would be
kept the same.

Now the leaves fall again on the backs of the cows,
and the ripe apples come underfoot. How the old
man stoops at his gate when I speak to him, drawing
answers from his pipe.

Already the moon is up, a full choir of light
on the old stone wall, where only one thief has leapt
in the long infallible memory of the parish, in the
late moonlight. The mist is not here on the
stone wall,

but in the valley the mist is a hovering promise.
Beat out your heart against relentless winter.
Say *It's going to be hard, this one* and love it
secretly.

Some Things

Some things I cannot leave behind:
children, husband, friends;
the smell of pine on the steep path
in the Schwartzwald,
where we met the old holzhacker
fixing the crucifix;
the bench by the chapel at the top
where the sun grinned down.

Salmon and garlic and sweet potatoes,
the crackle of almonds in the pan.

I am not an extinctionist,
I'm a fan of karma and reincarnation.
But how can I leave all this?

I will abscond with the priceless cameos
and extol all these things in heaven.
Death will not put its hand over my mouth.

The Earth Speaks in Tunis

1

'I love you so much,' she said.
'I will use every element to tell you.'

So the gold wind of the sirocco swirls
in the street, into nostrils and doorways.

The wild hair of the wind wraps
around lamps and palm trees, twining
with the night-black hair of the women.

North, by the sea, Sidi Bou Said,
proud of its palace, dreams of the fez.

And Carthage, its cousin,
keeps watch in the graveyard –
in its lap sleep Phoenicians and Greeks.

A young woman from England
lies roasting on the ruins
with a fever of 107,
delirious
in armoured company
and a babble of old tongues.

2

The earth spoke:
'South, in the desert,
the library of stones

holds the memory of aeons.
Drawers of cards with
the names of dinosaurs,

catalogues of ravages,
floods of love surging
from the souls of saints –

the stately parade of epochs
peoples your sleep.
I am awake

while you sleep, my children,
you sleep through your life
while I work.

In a dumb dense sleep
you are merciless to your brothers ...
that breaks my heart.

The number of times my heart breaks
must baffle the abacus.'

The Month of the Dead

The month of the dead
and the living rigid
at the onslaught of the cold.

Every year is the same:
the soul is a battlefield,
the mighty powers in deadlock.

Every year it is different:
the rain is new dead speaking,
weeping for our deafness,
their tenderness streaming –
and we nearly hear.

While the magpie
forages in the field,
and the red ferret
rifles below.

HELEN MOORE

Green Drift

There is no force in the world but love.

Rainer Maria Rilke

Crawling into bed like a peasant,
with mud-grained feet, soil under the nails
of my toes – but too tired to care –
the heaviness of the day's exertions draws

my body downward – each muscle and bone
finding its bliss – and I close my eyes
on a green panorama, shades of every
nuance, the contours of leaves in high

definition. A film encoded on the visual cortex,
I observe again those lanceolate shapes, the forage silk
which slipped between our fingers and thumbs
(still redolent with that Ramson scent),

the mounding herbage that we plucked,
backs bent as in a Van Gogh study.
Behind my eyelids, vernal waves rise and fall,
hymn of this community to which my senses flock –

ancient rite of magnetic birds, Dionysius riding me,
greens rushing on the inside of my eyelids,

mosaics of foliage, fingers ablaze with Nettle stings,
soles still alive to the narrow woodland path,

its vertebrae of roots, pad of compressed earth.
High on Spring, I'm a biophile
and incurable; nor would I care for any cure –
would only be a node in Great Mother's body

where, drifting into the canopy of sleep, I see foliar veins
close up – illumined as if by angels –
feel the breathing of stomata. Then, like a drunken Bee,
I surrender to this divine inebriation.

Modern Magus

Silbury Hill, 5 July 2009
for Ken

Cupped by the land, the massive Neolithic pap. From its peak, the
night-watch sees bubbles of light floating over the field. To the
modern magus, it's a sign of a supernatural circle, and the news is
instantly diffused, bounced off the satellites of cell phone corporations.
Dawn brings crocodilian aircraft droning overhead, snapping up
their aerial pix; more will follow with hordes of serial spotters.

On the ground, the form's hazy in our minds as we climb the
barbed-wire fence. In deference to the farmer's crop, the procession
ants through tram-lines cut in waves of regulated green (a hollow in
our hearts for Yellow Rattle, Cornflowers, Poppies).

At the threshold of the temple, the Sun beats the circle silver, and
the Skylarks offer molten jubilations. We bend to slip off shoes and

socks and feet flow over the bowed stems of corn, feel it thick as
rush matting – but this alone cannot explain these strange
sensations, tingling energy that electrifies our bodies.

Is this what brings us pilgrims? This frisson of mystery in a world
irrationally dogmatic? Devotees douse with rods or practise Chi
Gong; others sit in small vortices drumming and chanting into the
mystical tattoo. All around the corn wavers, twitching its ears.

In Good Hands

You see these, she says,
hands rising into the lamplight
from her shadowed lap,
their easy coupling
parted for a while –

palms up, her fingers stick out,
callused, knobbled at every joint,
like Willows pollarded for years.
In each hand's basin, lines with tributaries
are like streams viewed from high in the hills;
the backs speckled Blackbird eggs,
nails horned as Donkey's hooves.
Fearless hands that grasped Nettles
(*if you hold your breath they won't sting*);
that saved seeds, grubbed
in the woods for Pignuts;
picked Rosehips, Blackberries,
and never mind the scratches;
snipped Betony from the waysides,
slipping stems into mossy pockets,

to wind them out again, fresh as water
from a well. Those constant hands
that cored Liberty, Spartans, Pippins;
delved in dough; raced pies
from the oven; that fed the birds,
darned, soothed, rubbed olive oil
into the raw, new skins of babies;
made haphazard hospital corners;
put out huge House Spiders
and Small Tortoiseshells; laid Cowslips
on the graves of village people –

Like this. Her fingers interlock
to form the church without the steeple.
In our Earth everything fits together just so.
Wide-eyed I stared at their craggy surface
that settled back into her lap
as if in silent prayer. In good hands
I learned to cherish every living thing.

Time-out, Black-out

for Earth Hour

Sitting quietly as if no one were at home,
in candlelight our faces morph, shadows fly,
we breathe in the silence and our pulses slow,

unplug, disengaging from the charge that throws
the box, the red-eyed Cyclops off stand-by.
You and I are quiet, as if we were alone –

no phone, no gadgets, no kinetic motion
humming, whirring all the time –
and breathe in the silence till our pulses slow

the treadmill, at a standstill the revolving doors
so nothing moves, shut down all production lines.
We sit quietly, the ending unknown,

while across the land steely rows of scaffolds
no longer hold the buzz that plies our wires;
breathing in the silence our pulses slow,

the lights go out across the globe
as all the Earth respires.
We wait quietly, now very much at home;
breathing in the silence, our faces glow.

106

PAUL NELSON

Another Day Will Come

after Darwish

Another day will come, *feminine*
marvellous and tough, a whole system
jewel in the net of Indra, with a seventy
percent chance of sunbreaks. The newspaper
will search for homicides, suicides and find
none, but a healerwoman will find the cold
of a left foot and trigger a release of piezo-
electric energy as three ginkgo leaves spiral
onto the sidewalk in slow motion ... 'Extend
the dreamtime into Tuesday. Let the June
sun beam warmth onto your face and neck
while you look for the next omen. It will arrive
before you realise you're any older.'
Another day will come, *feminine, marvellous*
and tough as a block chord Monk might
play with a forearm. All future events
will have the female form as their guide,
menstrual blood will again flow from rocks.
Each will have their song their water their
own ritual to strengthen divinity. And a cat
will nap next to rusting rocket-launchers.

Sun

after Charles Olson

right in my eyes
7.15 a.m. December 29
arrives over the lake
a half globe
blaze   full
in the face
approaching skyscrapers
  rises above
glare in its
burst of morning warmth
right on me
morning orange hot
as December sun can be
informs me
of its message
it rises & I should
hear it say
stay warm, man
take this heat
& rise rise
like I do
rise up
& burn
burn as hard
as long
and as thick
as you can, man
burn through
bare trees
let your burn

bounce off city glass
steel and huge
lake waves
as the people
head for work
head for that
highest arc
sit at the top, keep
sending out
    December
flares hot orange,
colour cirrus
pink apricot salmon
take this warmth
rise up, man, rise up
&
burn

JENNIE POWELL

Tulip Tree

It's over now, drunken soliciting,
Seduction by pear, apple, cherry,
Giddy lilac, chestnut tossed and shaken,
Wild excesses, Beltane-coupling,
Crazed carnival of blossom dancing in the street,
Orgy of passion, foam-tipped ecstasy
Subsiding in exhaustion.
                            High above the pavement
Still messy from the orgasm of spring
The tulip tree gravely lifts her near-green sconces
Half-hidden by the leaves, and holds them steady
To honour a more private consummation:
An act of love that lasts all summer long.

Place

Even the thistledown
Drifting randomly
Will light on its place.

And some fell on stony ground –
Not a good place.

I remember the story
But what is it about?

We are not the seed
Fated to fall
Some well, most badly –
Blaming the Sower –

No, I am the place
Fertile ground
Secret garden
Battle site
Place of power –

Yes, I am the place.
Free thistledown, come here.

Ceremony for the Winter Solstice

The ground on which we stand is a huge circle,
Drumhead stretched on ink-black space,
Blank starless vault, sky like a sooted bowl
Reversed over us, and the dark far horizon
A jagged ring of mountains, or the diamonds
Patterning the endless flank of Ouroboros
The all-encircling snake.

                      Silently we gather
Grouped closely, seeking reassurance
In the dismaying absence of light.
Darkness is huge, all round and over us.
This night is a hanging blade.

Beyond the binding snake love knows no bounds,
Limitless source of all. But here on earth
Love's counterpoise is death; not to negate
But dancing-partner, matching step for step,
Inevitably to curb. We are met here to die,
And in the interval to celebrate
The death-stamped dance of love.

Death measures our birthright,
Shows us the scope of all we took for granted:
How gladly have you lived? How chosenly?
Life breathes in, gives us space.
Death breathes out, intensifies, distils,
Removes all superfluity, leaving essence.
Life makes us love. Death makes us passionate.
Passion is its gift
That carries us beyond the sphere of death.

We link hands in the dark
And move in line across the dancing-ground.

Evening Light

The river's surface still as mercury
Mirrors the evening light. Brighter than sky
It gathers and prolongs the timeless moment.
Only a vole heading for its burrow
Scurries silently across the luminous patch,
Barely breaking a ripple.

Absorbed beside her firepit in the gloom
The shrunken, bent old woman is still knitting
A yeasty swell of porridge-coloured wool
That overflows her lap to the earth floor.
She is one of three sisters. While she knits
The stream reflects the sky, the vole paddles home,
The blunt heavy damp-earth smells
Hang layered in the still air.

The second of the three is miserly.
Her spindle pays out less thread every year
So that the garment that once was ample
Is turning skimpy and tight-knit.
The third is self-effacing. She lurks in deepest shadow
Almost motionless. Only now and then
Firelight defines the edges of her shears
As she snips an earthquake or a hurricane.
Still the crone keeps knitting. Still the river
Reflects the evening sky. One more time
The vole arrives safely.

JAY RAMSAY

The Boreen

It runs off a road off another one you'd call a main road if you had to.

All the way past the tiny neighbouring farm to a dark green and white repainted gateway, a silent swathe of pine trees lead in as boreen becomes drive, past an old forever-beached wooden boat filled with earth and rocks with a giant hogweed for a mast.

Walking past it in the soft suspended summer twilight, leaving the fairy trees over your shoulder in the rising field, and down to where it begins again

two paces wide, with its grassed-over centre dotted with purple vetch and daisies – and fields you've never seen so wild either side, fields that go back to the beginning of time with their thick green rushes and yellow ragwort

but wait: what can you hear? Nothing but the air, nothing but the flies: no car, near or far, no house, no dog past the overhanging trees towards the little bending laneside glen

and you walk into a Silent World that was the world, the lost world found, and you found in it now

flanked by its overgrown uncut verge: its waist high grasses sown
with equisetum (green horsetails from the beginning), bog iris in its
rising green blades, strawberry flowering brambles pink as roses ...

till every step becomes your breathing, where you are the only
rhythmic sound, the shod soles of your feet on its dove-grey tarmac
covering

as you jump – a disturbed blackbird startling your heart with its
warning cry, its wings lifting out from under a tree, passing through
you –

and the tan brown coats of two horses grazing up to their bellies in
reed grass in their fine muscular bulk are as loud

in the silence you have come to, like your senses renewed again: and
you, animal-human, spiritual and mortal, Adam returning alone all
his life towards paradise, Adam without his name, baptised again in
the living silence that was the language we lost that is all your body
knows

and all that secretly breathes through it whispering your untold being

that walks this boreen and to a place that is off a road, off a road, off
a main road calling itself Your Life.

Co. Sligo

115

from Anamnesis – the Remembering of Soul

Written as poet in residence at St James's Church, Piccadilly (2005–6)

10

Surely, this is the time
to remember the earth we love
however lost it might seem –
and ask ourselves what does it mean
to stand by it?

All I am.
The sandy path always reaching upwards
through the sunlit dappled beeches …
pilgrims passing, as we dreamt them …

The grassy ridge edge opening, then higher
where St Martha's stands above the pines
and the way stretches on into the misty beyond.

It was the journey, its romance and mystery
all that life could ever be –
and it was belonging, that could let me
walk anywhere and feel the land
as one story, in all its memory
grounding our deeper reality –

And to stand by that
for the best we can be
in spite of our insanity

is to obey that unanswerable command,
and *walk in beauty*.

11

They, you, I, we
are killing God's creation

for one reason only
fear, masked as greed.

They long for painless immunity
heaven on earth
in their schizoid fortresses
without looking to see
the desert their money is farmed in.

No: I, you, we are blind.
Give us eyes. Give us eyes in time.

Albatross, bonobo, corncockle, eidelweiss
lynx, monk seal, po'o-uli, Tuvalu ...

and will they rise in a higher dimension
folded back into the Universal Mind
to be reborn again at the right time –

Can we afford to believe it?

No, and yes: in what it means
to let the Dream of Life take us
always further on to where
the sun is really shining,
the moon is magic and bright

as we walk on the Summerland island
hearing the abbey bell ring.

Driving Home, Christmas Day

for my father (d. 2007)

You can live half your life in a fantasy of yourself
but then it suddenly becomes vital not to lie
about where you came from and who you are
through those who made you, behind you –
because, however difficult they were, they are
your only ground where the earth bisects
your vertical being and becoming ...

Whoever you have behind you, don't discard them
being true to who you are, but in seeing them, see
they are the love you have to prove
in this river you've been born into
reaching from your tree into its only roots.

So as I see you sitting in the light and smiling,
in your cream polo neck, watery blue-eyed, I know
that only the truth allows the love to be
its shining fullness, allowing me to receive
its strength and blessing, seeing me on my way tonight.
and every night I'll go on leaving you
to cross this void of darkness outside –

arriving a little deeper into the mystery
of the life that was given to be mine.

If the Grass Could Speak in Her Voice

and because it does

Swim into my cool dew depths, hurrying man
and don't be afraid of the weeds
or of losing your breath.
                    You can see
down here too, dark as it is …

I am all that is holding you.

Flat out on the evening grass,
this is who you are at last.

Open air womb, and mother, skin –
to be with your sisters and brothers.
You are all children grown in the sun
and earth is where you live, twice born

your journey inside the marrow of Creation.

There is no other ground
and you are always returning …

sleeping, eating, swooning, dreaming.

If you lose me, you lose your soul.

I am the green voice you cannot command.

I am the love you will live to fulfil.

In Bowood Library

for Joanna and Izzy
Bowood House, near Calne, Wilts.

The flattened skin as if ironed without a crease
to the edge of the claws and the tail, lifeless in 2D
at the centre, in front of the fireplace: jaws, sabre teeth
wedged open under taxidermist's eyes
for fierceness – to rationalise
the murder that was yours, for sport,
for proof of our pathetic domination.

Your leonine hide stretched like savannah,
the earth from the air, where gazelle and zebra
and wildebeest cross and pink flamingos
cloud above wherever there is water
but there's none here, only dry musty leatherbound
books on the rising shelves; with their soporific smell
in the afterlunch haze … and above them
painted into the ceiling's moulding, in relief,
the faces of the Greek philosophers in profile
impassive as vases.

So we ruled
and now we pay the price

and as we stand to leave, to breathe the sunlight,
the alarm goes off … as the suspects exit,
breaking the trance of centuries.

LYNNE WYCHERLEY

The Substitute Sky

Each day we stare at screens,
a sly fluorescence, a not-quite sky
where swarms of data
aggregate and fly

while unseen cloud-and-sunlight
walks the grass, gold shoes
then grey, and beech and oak,
the green-leaved angels, pray.

Pilots of pixel storms,
what do we bring? Less talk,
less laughter, less sun on our skins;
our lives on hold, our children wired in.

Core addiction: captive eyes.
Outside the real world breathes, and dies.

Corncrakes

Child of the uncut meadows,
the hand-reaped hay,
black chicks growing to rust and gold,
night to day, alchemical,

felled from England, gone
to the blade. Corncrake sing:
our driven world has driven you
to this edge. Papa Westray,
an Orkney ledge
lush with grass, a living weave,
a bird-rich stone in the sea.

Corncrake sing: don't follow
the last auk over the cliff.
What savvy we have still lives here,
its seed lifting slowly to the sun

while ego-us is lost in its toys –
sat-nav, podcasts, MP3s

and you, wisdom, and the weave decline:
a barren planet, a burning rind.

Britain's last great auk was shot from a boat off Papa Westray

Cloudberries

Search for them
on upland peat,
a sphagnum pelt
where rocks graze sky
and reindeer
scuttle the air
with quick sounds,
ghosting away
from your scent.

Yellow berries,
midsummer beads,
distillates
of the sleepless north
when day never sets.

Tread with care:
there is joy and grief
to find such light
in the loneliness

as if the sun had seen us
and had wept.

Littoral

Now the sun opens
its luminous book
and pages fan
in the long-fingered breeze,
marram grass, fennel,
the tide's running glaze.

Blue trails through blue,
turquoise, metallic hues,
and the soul
rediscovers itself
in tourmaline,
sapphire, beryline –

frost-tips of ling,
wave-crests
of bracken –
white gull on the wing,
its outstretched shadow
caressing the sand

without touching.

Sea Walls

Tonight: a night so clear,
a blue frost burns the air.
It strips the stars naked;
its silence scours the hills

dissolves the sea-walls
we build around mystery, eggshells
of concrete and tempered steel,
the thimbles we hide in.

Now I too close curtains,
lock starlight in glass,
take shelter in ego's small drop,
tabletop certainties

a lamp's yellow glade
but even here, splitting
its star in a three-inch pot,
a primrose mouths immensities.

AN ECOBARDIC AFTERWORD

The shift in collective consciousness that Jay Ramsay invokes, in his introduction, as necessary to our response to the deepening crisis in our relationship with the ecosystem has implications for all aspects of human culture. In *An Ecobardic Manifesto* (Awen, 2008), Fire Springs called for a paradigm shift in the arts: an approach to making and valuing art which acknowledges and responds to this central challenge of our time. The existence of such a movement matters more than its name, but we had to call it something, so we called it 'ecobardic', since key elements of our inspiration emerged from the bardic tradition of training, composition, and performance. On the core premise of responsiveness to the strained relationship between human beings and the rest of nature, we elucidated five ecobardic principles: (1) to triangulate one's existence in past, present, and future time and the particularity and diversity of place; (2) to offer cultural leadership in the midst of an oceanic flood of trivial information; (3) to honour one's audience as a creative partner; (4) to foster a sense of beauty in the world by means of the well-wrought craft of one's art; and (5) to re-enchant nature and people's lives as filled with significance.

In identifying these principles, we did not want to lay down a prescriptive programme. For a paradigm shift to take place on the scale that seems necessary, there needs to be a vast diversity of creative initiatives and responses, that touch different kinds of people and impart different kinds of effect: countless different streams of creativity that will flow together as a great current carrying our civilisation in a constructive and hopeful direction rather than deeper into the maelstrom of ecological and economic breakdown. In recognising a sense of a *movement* in the arts, those of us working in this field may find encouragement, inspiration, the strength of common cause.

Soul of the Earth is a delightful manifestation of such a movement, not just in the quality of the individual contributions but in that it brings *together* an array of poets of fine calibre who each in their own way gives voice to particular and very diverse nuances of our relationship with the natural world to which we belong and yet from which we are, in various ways, alienated.

The ecobardic principle of 're-enchantment' is the part of the Ecobardic Manifesto where we open the door to the possibility of the spiritual. This is a tricky territory, since many see the religious traditions as unhelpful to the challenges we now face, and at the same time the scale of the challenges requires cooperation between those who call themselves spiritual and those who sincerely deny there's any reality beyond that which can be interrogated by science. The poetry in this book is presented as 'eco-spiritual'. Whether you conceive of the spiritual in brazenly metaphysical terms – as a Christian, a Druid, a Buddhist will – or in a more psychological way, these poems invite a heightened sense of the significance of what we see around us and of the significance of the very act of perceiving. The sense of 'and more' in everything. There are many fine examples here of poems that, for me, deliver the kind of 'ecopoetic' effect that Jonathan Bate elucidates in *The Song of the Earth* (Macmillan, 2001): the poem imaginatively transports you into an intimate experience of some facet of nature and does so in such a way that you feel the desire to experience nature more fully in lived experience, and that your sensibilities are sharpened to appreciate things you might not otherwise have noticed, and, crucially, that you feel a heightened regard – what I would call 'love' – for the well-being of those things of nature.

This is why the re-enchantment of nature matters. In perceiving a greater significance in something you feel a heightened empathy towards it. More and more it seems to me that the cultivation of empathy towards the other – the other person, the other group, the other nation, the non-human other in nature – is utterly fundamental to our hopes for the planet. We may devise super-efficient photoelectric cells to provide a new stream of energy, we may count the populations of each endangered species, we may draw up treaties to define the rights of disadvantaged people, but if we have not love we are nothing. Someone who's chosen to read a book of poems may be expected to be susceptible to Bate's ecopoetic effect. But, if we're honest, we have to admit that a large proportion of people, even in a country so privileged as Britain, stand outside the sphere of influence of poetry experienced in such a private meditative way, or indeed in the conventional poetry-reading event. Jay Ramsay has long been on a mission to expose wider audiences to poetry that does not compromise the gravity of its content. Here the 'bardic' part of 'ecobardic' comes into play. Many of the contributors to *Soul of the Earth* are adept at performing their work; to do so is an integral part of their identity as poets. A number of them – like Gabriel Millar ('poems, like love-talk, should go from mouth to ear') – habitually memorise their poems to perform them without reading. It's not as superhuman a feat as people sometimes think; actors and singers routinely learn their lines and no one seems amazed by that. But the benefit to communication with the audience is huge. Learning your work *by heart* compels you to circulate its meaning more deeply *within* your heart, to become in a sense more deeply acquainted with what you have created. I witnessed this most powerfully, over a period of years, in the development of the late Mary Palmer's confidence and impact in performing her poetry. Divested of the defence of books and papers, the poet stands vulnerable before their audience. Their words come not mediated from the page but straight from the heart, speak directly to the audience, and the very vulnerability deepens the authenticity of whatever the poems share.

In the performance situation, too, other kinds of ecobardic impact become possible besides the kind of effect that Bate describes. Some poems – Aidan Andrew Dun's 'Treadwell' might be an example in this book – when publicly performed make a polemic impact, that challenges, confronts, yet it's a kind of polemic that, like a finely wrought tool or weapon, is refined to a high degree of precision and penetrative power by a poet's unique skill with words. More numerous in this eco-spiritual anthology are poems – such as ones by Rose Flint and Irina Kuzminsky – that have an incantatory quality that might suit them to employment in a ritual context, where the listeners are not merely listeners but active participants who deliberately open themselves to the possibility of some transformation of spirit.

Whatever the particular context in which poetry is spoken, whatever the particular impact of the poem, in public performance the poetry is shared and received collectively. There's the possibility that any transformative effect it might have may be collective, relational, rather than individual. This brings us back to the necessity of cooperation, however trying we may find that; of getting along together on this lovely but troubled planet in whatever networks of collaboration we can sustain. This book, *Soul of the Earth*, is in its own modest way the fruit of such cooperation among all those who've contributed to its creation.

Anthony Nanson

THE CONTRIBUTORS

Poet, author, and painter **Roselle Angwin** leads the Fire in the Head creative and reflective writing programme. Her work hinges on inner and outer geographies: the connections between self and Self, self and other, self and place, and creativity and well-being. She has been described as 'a poet of the bright moment ... whose own sources of creative inspiration are her native Westcountry, the Scottish islands, and a highly individual blend of Celtic metaphysics, psychology, shamanic and Buddhist thinking'. She is a passionate champion of wild places and the environment, and leads Ground of Being work on Dartmoor, on Iona, and abroad.

Aidan Andrew Dun is a poet, composer, and psychogeographer. His exploration of the mysteries of Kings Cross in the epic *Vale Royal* (Goldmark, 1995, launched at the Albert Hall) caused a groundswell of interest in this extraordinary zone of London. *Universal* (Goldmark, 2002, launched at City Lights) is set in India, the West Indies, and Morocco. *The Uninhabitable City* (Goldmark), a collection of short poems, appeared in 2005; *Salvia Divinorum* (Goldmark), an alchemical text in four movements, in 2007. *McCool* (Goldmark, 2010), a verse novel in nearly 300 rhyming sonnets, has its background in London and Lebanon and is the story of a love triangle set against world conflagration and the 'clash of civilisations'. Aidan performs his work with the magical Czech pianist Lucie Rejchrtova. Grooves, impressionistic Satie-esque soundscapes support the words of a man who has been called a Blakean messenger. They have performed in London, Amsterdam, Prague, and Paris.

Diana Durham is the author of three poetry collections – *Sea of Glass* (Diamond Press, 1990), *To the End of the Night* (winner of Northwoods Press's 2003 competition), and *Between Two Worlds: A Series of Sonnets* (Chrysalis Poetry, 2014) – the non-fiction *The Return of King Arthur* (Tarcher/Penguin, 2004), and a novel, *The Curve of the Land* (Skylight Press, 2015). Her poetry has featured in numerous anthologies and journals in the UK and USA, including *Orbis* and *Parabola*. Diana was a member of the London poetry performance group Angels of Fire, with whom she appeared at the Royal Festival Hall's Voice Box. In New Hampshire she founded 3 Voices: three women writers who received state funding and performed state-wide. Diana has also written, performed, and co-produced an audio-drama retelling of the grail myth entitled *Perceval & the Grail*. She presents on the meaning of the Grail/Arthur myths.

Karen Eberhardt-Shelton was born in northern California, moved to England in her teens, divided time between the UK and the US over many years (became an English citizen in the 1960s), and has resided in various other parts of the world. While living in Stroud, Gloucestershire, she wrote a weekly column for the *Stroud News & Journal*. Her current home is in Wales. *The Message* (David Paul), poetry with Jay Ramsay, was published in 2002. Her anthology *A Women's Guide to Saving The World* (Book Guild) appeared in 2008 and is due to be republished. An autobiographical book, *To Camelot, with Love*, is in press. Her major concerns now revolve around global issues, particularly overpopulation, and her current project is 'Awesome Earth Education: How Can We Change the Way People Think?'

Rose Flint is a writer and artist therapist. She works with poetry in healthcare and is Lead Writer for the Kingfisher Project, working in the community and hospital of Salisbury. A committed environmentalist, she uses awareness of the natural world as a way of engaging with the health and well-being of the individual, believing that the health of the world and of each one of us is ultimately linked. She is an award-winning poet, her prizes including the Cardiff International and the Petra Kenney Poetry Competitions. She has published five collections of poetry: *Blue Horse of Morning* (Seren, 1992), *Nekyia* (Stride, 2003), *Firesigns* (Poetry Salzburg, 2004), *Mother of Pearl* (PS Avalon, 2008), and *A Prism for the Sun* (Oversteps, 2015). Her poetry is regularly published in *We'Moon*, the American goddess yearbook, and many British magazines, including *Poetry Review*, *Scintilla*, *Resurgence*, and *Acumen*.

Dawn Gorman devises and runs arts and literary events, including the reading series Words & Ears in Bradford on Avon, with Arts Council support in 2015. As a poet she collaborates with the Orchestra of the Age of Enlightenment, who have written a symphony based on her poem *Replenishment*; her film poem of the same name appeared at Cannes Short Film Festival in 2015. In collaboration with ceramicist Liz Watts, she was poet in residence at the EDS Gallery in Edinburgh during the Fringe (2015, 2016) and is poet in residence at Greenhill Cottage Gallery in Southwick, Wiltshire. Her work is published in anthologies including *The Book of Love and Loss* (Belgrave Press, 2014), *Salt on the Wind* (Elephantsfootprint, 2016), and a centenary celebration of Bath's Holburne Museum (2016), and in literary journals including *The Interpreter's House* and *Iota*. Her pamphlet *This Meeting of Tracks* was published by Toadlily Press in 2013.

Alyson Hallett is a prize-winning poet whose collections include *On Ridgegrove Hill* (Atlantic Press, 2015), *Suddenly Everything* (Poetry Salzburg, 2013), and *The Stone Library* (Peterloo Poets, 2007). She has also published fiction, written drama for BBC Radio 4 and Sky Television, and undertaken many collaborative projects with artists. She has a poem carved into Milsom Street pavement in Bath and curates an ongoing project on poetry as public art, The Migration Habits of Stones. Alyson grew up in Street, Somerset. Her childhood was infused with Clarks' shoe factory where her father and sister worked, a view of Glastonbury Tor, and the lattice of rhynes that criss-cross the Levels. She studied comparative literature at the University of East Anglia, gained an MA in creative writing from Bath Spa University, and has completed a practice-based PhD. Alyson is an advisory fellow with the Royal Literary Fund and is working on her next book of poems.

Jeremy Hooker grew up in Warsash near Southampton and at Pennington, on the edge of the New Forest, and the landscapes of this region have remained an important source of inspiration. Many of his poems were written in Wales, where he has lived for long periods. His academic career has taken him to universities in England, the Netherlands, and the USA. He is now Emeritus Professor of the University of South Wales. Besides his eleven collections of poetry represented in *The Cut of the Light* (Enitharmon, 2006), Jeremy is well known as a critic and has published selections of writings by Edward Thomas and Richard Jefferies, and studies of David Jones and John Cowper Powys, all of them important to his own creative life. Other critical titles include *Writers in a Landscape* (University of Wales Press, 1996) and *Imagining Wales* (University of Wales Press, 2001), while *Welsh Journal* (Seren, 2001) records his life in Wales during the 1970s, and *Upstate: A North American Journal* (Shearsman, 2007) a period in upstate New York. His most recent books are *Openings: A European Journal* (Shearsman, 2014) and a new collection of poems, *Scattered Light* (Enitharmon, 2015).

Adam Horovitz is a poet, journalist, and editor. He was born in 1971 in London and raised in Gloucestershire. He has read at events such as Glastonbury Festival and Cheltenham Literature Festival and took part in the inaugural Days of Poetry and Wine Festival in Slovenia in 1996. His poetry has appeared in magazines such as *Acumen*, *Tears in the Fence*, *SAW*, *Tellus*, *Fourth World Review*, *Hand + Star*, *Salt's Horizon Review*, and *New Departures* and in a number of anthologies, including *The Orange Dove of Fiji* (Hutchinson, 1989), *Oral* (Sceptre, 1999), *Asking a Shadow to Dance* (Oxfam DVD, 2009), and *The Listening Shell* (Headland, 2010). He was poet in residence for Glastonbury Festival website in 2009. He is the author of the acclaimed poem collection *Turning* (Headland, 2011) and the memoir *A Thousand Laurie Lees* (History Press, 2014).

Charlotte Hussey wrote her doctorate on the twentieth-century poet H.D., who shared her interest in antiquity. Her MFA in poetry allowed her to undertake an in-depth study of Yeats's metrical practices, which equipped her to tackle a collection of glosas, entitled *Glossing the Spoils* (Awen, 2012). Charlotte is a Celtic shaman, belly dancer, and creativity coach. She teaches creative writing, Old Irish myths and tales, Arthurian literature, and a creativity course at Montreal's Dawson College. Her poetry has appeared in Canada, the United States, and Britain. She has also published *Rue Sainte Famille* (Vehicule, 1991), which was shortlisted for the QSPELL awards, and a chapbook, *The Head Will Continue to Sing*.

Irina Kuzminsky is a poet, dancer, and singer who passionately believes in the arts as a bridge into spiritual consciousness. Born in Australia into a White Russian émigré family, she won a scholarship to Oxford, where she wrote her doctorate on the 'Language of Women' and was elected Junior Research Fellow in Humanities at Wolfson College. She is the author of *Dancing with Dark Goddesses* (Awen, 2009), *light muses* (with artist Jan Delaney, Naditu Press, 2011), *Into the Silence* (Chrysalis, 2016), and poems and articles in *Esoteric Quarterly*, *Acumen*, *Caduceus*, *Poetrix*, *Poetry Chaikhana*, and elsewhere. As Irinushka she has released three CDs of her poetry set to music: *Would That I Could* (2010), *Roads Travelled* (2014), and *Orpheus Sings* (2016). Her one-woman show *Dancing with Dark Goddesses* has been seen in New York, Melbourne, Germany, and the UK. Her art is centred in spiritual feminism; poetry, dance, and music being central to her life's journey into the divine feminine.

Kevan Manwaring is the author of The Windsmith Elegy series of novels (Awen, 2004–12), *The Bardic Handbook* (Gothic Image, 2006), *Desiring Dragons* (Compass Books, 2014), *Lost Islands* (Heart of Albion Press, 2008), *The Way of Awen* (O Books, 2010), *Oxfordshire Folk Tales* (History Press, 2012), *Northamptonshire Folk Tales* (History Press, 2013), and *The Immanent Moment* (Awen, 2010). A substantial gathering of his bardic verse, *Silver Branch*, is forthcoming from Awen. A Fellow of Hawthornden, the Eccles Centre (British Library), and the Higher Education Academy, Kevan has taught creative writing for the Open University since 2004, as well as at Portsmouth University, Imperial College London, and Skyros Writers' Lab. He writes for the *London Magazine* and is a co-judge of their short story competition. He was a consultant for BBC TV's *The Secret Life of Books*. Based in Stroud, Gloucestershire, he tweets and blogs as 'The Bardic Academic'.

Paul Matthews lives in Forest Row, Sussex. For many years he has taught creative writing and gymnastics at Emerson College. He also travels widely, speaking his poetry and encouraging others in the use of imagination through the interactive workshops that he offers. His inspirational books on the creative process – *Words in Place* (2007) and *Sing Me the Creation* (available from 2015 in a new and improved second edition) – are both published by Hawthorn Press. *The Ground that Love Seeks* (Five Seasons Press, 1996) and *Slippery Characters* (Five Seasons Press, 2011) are gatherings of his poetry..

Margie McCallum now lives in her homeland of Aotearoa New Zealand after a transformative decade in the UK. It was during her time in the UK that she encountered a plea for expression from the poet inside; she credits Jay Ramsey and Rosie Jackson with aiding her response to that. Margie's poetry spans many topics, perhaps finding its clearest and most resonant voice in response to landscape or in the face of death. *When Death Comes Close* (Museday, 2010) is a CD and booklet of poems arising from Margie's personal and professional experiences around death, dying, and funerals. Rose Flint writes, 'These are poems that bridge earth and spirit. Luminous and gentle, they both soften loss and honour the strength of its place within our lives.' Margie also enjoys painting, conversations that delve deep, and walking the long beach near her home.

Jehanne Mehta is a singer, songwriter, and poet who has been writing poems since childhood and songs since her twenties. She has had four books of poetry published and six albums of songs recorded. The latest album, *This Place,* came out in 2015. Her writing, emerging from her own inner journey, is committed to transformation and is a plea to awaken to our inner selves and to the Earth. She has three grown-up children and lives in Gloucestershire with her husband and musical partner, Rob.

Gabriel Bradford Millar is a renegade American, born in New York in 1944. She spent five years at universities in New York and Edinburgh, where she published in *Lines Review* and *Scottish International,* read on BBC TV, and was interviewed by George Bruce on BBC Radio Scotland. She married an Englishman, raised children and chickens in Gloucestershire, and taught English at a Steiner school. Outposts published *Mid-Day* in 1977; then came *The Brook Runs* and *Bloom on the Stone. Thresholds: Near-Life Experiences* (Hawthorn Press) came out in 1995. Forty years of poetry are distilled in *The Saving Flame* (Five Seasons Press, 2001) and *Crackle of Almonds* (Awen, 2012). Gabriel has given scores of readings and over a hundred playshops and, with Jay Ramsay, co-founded Poetry Stroud and Celebration of the Word as forums for other poets. She believes that poems, like love-talk, should go from mouth to ear, without any paper in between.

Helen Moore is an award-winning ecopoet and socially engaged artist based in Somerset. Her debut poetry collection, *Hedge Fund, and Other Living Margins* (Shearsman, 2012), was described by Alasdair Paterson as being 'in the great tradition of visionary politics in British poetry'. Her second collection, *ECOZOA* (Permanent, 2015), which responds to Thomas Berry's vision of the 'Ecozoic Era', has already been acclaimed by John Kinsella as 'a milestone in the journey of ecopoetics'. *Greenspin*, a video-poem Helen made with film-maker Howard Vause, which exposes the language of corporate advertising and greenwashing, won third prize in the Liberated Words International Poetry Film Festival in 2013.

Anthony Nanson teaches creative writing at Bath Spa University and has performed widely as a storyteller. He's the author of *Storytelling and Ecology* (Society for Storytelling, 2005), *Exotic Excursions* (Awen, 2008), award-winning *Words of Re-enchantment* (Awen, 2011) and *Gloucestershire Folk Tales* (History Press, 2012), and the novel *Deep Time* (Hawthorn Press, 2015); also a co-editor of *Storytelling for a Greener World* (Hawthorn Press, 2014) and co-author of *An Ecobardic Manifesto* (Awen, 2008) and *Gloucestershire Ghost Tales* (History Press, 2015). He was the editor of *Artyfact* from 1997 to 2001 and became the publisher of Awen in 2015.

Paul Nelson is a poet, interviewer, and essayist. He founded Seattle Poetics LAB and the Cascadia Poetry Festival and has written *American Sentences* (Apprentice House, 2015), *A Time Before Slaughter* (Apprentice House, 2009, shortlisted for a 2010 Genius Award by *The Stranger*), Organic Poetry (VDM Verlag, 2008), and *Organic in Cascadia: A Sequence of Energies* (Lumme Editions, 2013). He's interviewed Allen Ginsberg, Michael McClure, Sam Hamill, José Kozer, Robin Blaser, Nate Mackey, Joanne Kyger, George Bowering, Brenda Hillman, and Daphne Marlatt, presented poetry/poetics in London, Brussels, Nanaimo, Qinghai, Beijing, has had work translated into Spanish, Chinese, Portuguese, and writes an American Sentence every day. Awarded a residency at The Lake, from the Morris Graves Foundation in Loleta, CA, he's published work in *Golden Handcuffs Review, Zen Monster, Hambone,* and elsewhere. Winner of the 2014 Robin Blaser Award from the *Capilano Review*, he lives in the Duwamish River watershed.

136

Jennie Powell was born in Glasgow in 1938 but moved to London in time to encounter the personal growth movement and the alternative scene. She studied traditional Chinese medicine and briefly practised in this before finding her poetic calling towards the end of her professional life. Now resident in Gloucestershire, she is moved to write by her natural surroundings and shamanic journeys. Her collection of poems *The Grain in the Wood* was published by the Lotus Foundation in 2004 and her work has appeared in several anthologies.

Jay Ramsay has been an influential presence on the poetry scene over the last thirty years and has come into his own as a voice for transformative spiritual, political, and psychological awareness. Described as 'England's foremost transformation poet' (*Caduceus*), he believes that poetry has a unique catalytic role. He is the author, translator, or editor of over thirty books of poetry and non-fiction. Most recently: *Monuments* (Waterloo Press, 2014), *Shu Jing: The Book of History* (Penguin Classics, 2014), *Places of Truth: Journeys into Sacred Wilderness* (Awen, new edition 2016), as well as *The Poet in You* (O Books, 2009), which publishes part of his Chrysalis poetry correspondence course (established 1990). Forthcoming is *Dreams Down Under*, a sequence about Australia (knivesforksandspoons, 2016). Poetry editor of *Caduceus* magazine since 2002, he is a UKCP-accredited psychosynthesis psychotherapist and healer in private practice in Stroud and London, where he also runs monthly men's groups.

Lynne Wycherley writes, 'At depth, all my poetry is a kind of love poetry, whether for people or places, wild creatures, or stars … It is also a rebellion against reductionism: light, both metaphysical and physical, permeates my imagination and my words.' Widely published, she has been voted an 'Alternative Generation Poet' (*Staple*); her prizes include (she blushes) the 2009 Fellows' Poetry Prize (English Association). Her *Listening to Light: New & Selected Poems* was published in 2014 by Shoestring Press. She is currently a health refugee in Devon, working to raise awareness of the suppressed risks associated with the wireless boom – to children, ecology, and ourselves.

ACKNOWLEDGEMENTS

The editor and contributors would like to thank the publishers and editors of the publications in which some of these poems have been published. All poems are used by permission of their authors.

Roselle Angwin. 'Earth Heart Days' is also published in *Confluence: Poetry from the Two Rivers group*, ed. Roselle Angwin, Leaf Books, Abercynon, 2010.

Rose Flint. 'Prayer for Always Peace', 'Running on Empty', 'Field of Light', 'Sedna at Tadusack', and 'Another World Is Possible' were first published in *Mother of Pearl*, PS Avalon, Glastonbury, 2008.

Dawn Gorman. 'Holy Well' and 'Quarry' were first published in *Looking for Gods*, Community of Poets and Artists Press, 1998.

Jeremy Hooker. 'To the Unknown Labourer', 'Nobbut Dick Jefferies', and 'Landscape of the Daylight Moon' were published in *Landscape of the Daylight Moon* (Enitharmon Press, 1978). 'Walking All Day in the Forest' was published in *Their Silence a Language* (Enitharmon Press, 1993). 'Cyane' was published in *Adamah* (Enitharmon Press, 2002). All the poems appear in *The Cut of the Light: Poems 1965–2005*, Enitharmon Press, London, 2006.

Paul Matthews. 'To the Lady', 'A Green Theology', and 'Carrying Language into a Wood' were first published in *The Ground that Love Seeks*, Five Seasons Press, Hereford, 1996.

Jehanne Mehta. 'Albion?' and 'Hymn to the Earth' were first published in *Cygnus Review*, July and September 2010. 'Nothing Now Common' was first published in *Walking Two Ways*, letterpress-printed limited edition, 2006.

Gabriel Bradford Millar. 'The Fere', 'Am I Ready?', 'Pitchcombe', and 'The Month of the Dead' were first published in *The Saving Flame*, Five Seasons Press, Hereford, 2001.

Jay Ramsay. 'The Boreen' was first published in *Scintilla*, No. 8, 2004. 'Driving Home, Christmas Day' was first published in *Out of Time: Poems 1998–2008* (PSAvalon, 2008). *Anamnesis* was published by Lotus Foundation, London, 2008.

Lynne Wycherley. 'The Substitute Sky' was first published in *This Life on Earth*, ed. Dinah Livingstone, Sea of Faith Network, Newcastle upon Tyne, 2009. 'Corncrakes' and 'Sea Walls' were first published in *North Flight*, Shoestring Press, Nottingham, 2006. 'Cloudberries' was first published in *Acumen*, No. 43, 2002.

All efforts have been taken to obtain details of previous publication. The publisher would welcome any further information.

The quotation on p. v is from Mary Palmer, 'Taliesin's Salmon', in *Tidal Shift*, ed. Jay Ramsay, Awen, Bath, 2009, pp. 22–3.

PUBLISHER'S NOTE

When I published *Soul of the Earth* in 2010, it felt like the culmination of the small press I'd started in 2003. Awen's first book, *Writing the Land: an anthology of natural words*, was the outcome of a course I ran on 'creative writing and the environment' at Envolve, Bath's environment centre. It was a group effort: I encouraged the students to contribute not only their words, but also to the editorial, design, and marketing process. Our modest vessel was joined by a number of more established writers, and I am pleased that familiar names from back then reappear in this later anthology. When *Soul of the Earth* was launched at a splendid event in Waterstones, I felt conscious of how far we, as a press, had come (in our craft; in our thinking) and how far we, as a species, still had to go (in our collective effort to live in more sustainable, harmonious ways).

As I write this the world looks in even worse shape than it did then. Not only are rapacious ideologies and practices continuing to damage this precious Earth (so much so that this epoch may be designated the 'Anthropocene' because of the lasting legacy we will leave in the Earth's fossil record because of our massive impact upon the biosphere), but humanity seems intent on tearing itself apart. Conflict in the Middle East, in Africa, in Eastern Europe, and elsewhere continues to create human suffering on a massive scale. The war in Syria has resulted in the migration of millions. The European project is fracturing. Right-wing extremism is on the march once again. Campaigners lobby for the closure of borders, for breaking away from the EU, for increasing parochialism. With such a bunker mentality, with selfishness, fear and loathing, and a perpetual heightened state of terror becoming the 'new normal', it is perhaps more poignant than ever to think of ourselves as 'souls of the earth'.

The title I came up with for this collection, finely curated by Jay Ramsay, seems increasingly resonant. Perhaps we need to have the perspective of British astronaut Tim Peake on the International Space Station and remember what unites us: the sheer unlikeliness and precariousness of our existence on this fragile blue jewel. To remember our common humanity. If I may paraphrase the Caribbean poet Derek Walcott: the only nation is the imagination. We can choose hope or despair. Perhaps, rather than allowing ourselves to be paralysed by the magnitude of what we face, we should reframe it as a 'call to adventure'. Rather than leaving a legacy of environmental denudation, of ecological catastrophe, of mass extinction, why not a fossil record of artistic activity? We need to live here and now, of course. And ensure the planet is left in a better condition. But it is also wise to take the long view and hope that what will survive of us will be the love we lived by: for each other, the planet, and all that lives upon it.

With that wish we cast this message in a bottle into the ocean. May this new edition find sympathetic shores. And we do hope you will spread the word. If you believe in our vision, please spend a few minutes to share reviews, comments, and thoughts about the book through whatever medium you revel in. Words matter and, combined with meaningful deeds, can help to make a difference.

Kevan Manwaring

www.awenpublications.co.uk

Also available from Awen Publications:

An Ecobardic Manifesto
Fire Springs

What is the raison d'être of the arts in an age of global ecological crisis? In this audacious document, Fire Springs present a new vision for the arts, one that holds together commitment to artistic integrity and craftsmanship with responsiveness to the peculiar challenges of our time. Foremost among those challenges are the strained relationship between human beings and the ecosystem we inhabit and the vital need to sustain empathy for that which is other than ourselves. Fundamental to the arts' task in such an age is a willingness to embrace contradiction, not least the deepening polarisation between scientific and economic materialism and metaphysical sources of meaning and hope. This pamphlet is a clarion call to everyone working in the arts today who wants their efforts to make a difference.

Art Theory/Literary Criticism   ISBN 978-1-906900-07-6   £2.50

Places of Truth:
journeys into sacred wilderness
Jay Ramsay

Poet and psychotherapist Jay Ramsay has been drawn to wild places all his writing life, in search of a particular deep listening experience. 'Trwyn Meditations', a sequence set in Snowdonia, begins this 24-year odyssey. 'By the Shores of Loch Awe' takes us to the fecund wilds of Scotland. 'The Oak' celebrates an ancient tree in the heart of the Cotswolds. 'The Sacred Way' is an evocation of Pilgrim Britain. 'Culbone' records the hidden history of the smallest parish church in England in a steep North Somerset valley near where Coleridge wrote 'Kubla Khan'. The final sequences, 'The Mountain' and 'Sinai', takes us beyond, in all senses, touching the places where we find I and Self.

'Beautiful, resonant, real and layered' *Peter Owen Jones*

Poetry ISBN 978-1-906900-40-3 £12.00
Spirit of Place Volume 4

Crackle of Almonds: selected poems
Gabriel Bradford Millar

In these renegade poems ranging from 1958 to 2011 Gabriel Bradford Millar presents a spectrum of life, in all its piquant poignancy, with unfaltering precision, defiance, and finesse. From the very first to the very last, the breathtaking skill of this consummate wordsmith does not waver. Many of the poems linger in the air – not least because Millar performs them orally with such verve. She believes 'that poems, like love-talk, should go from mouth to ear without any paper in between'. On the page their orality and aurality fragrance their presence without diminishing their literary elegance. Continually astonishing, these epicurean poems not only offer a lasting testimony to a 'life well-lived', but inspire the reader to live well too

'She does not just write *about* the world; she dips her syllables in the bitter sweet of its "gazpacho". She thinks melodically.' *Paul Matthews*

Poetry ISBN 978-1-906900-29-8 £9.99

Dancing with Dark Goddesses: movements in poetry
Irina Kuzminsky

The dance is life – life is the dance – in all its manifestations, in all its sorrow and joy, cruelty and beauty. And the faces of the Dark Goddesses are many – some are dark with veiling and unknowing, some are dark with sorrow, some are dark with mystery and a light so great that it paradoxically shades them from sight. The poems in this collection are an encounter with many of these faces, in words marked with feminine energy and a belief in the transformative power of the poetic word. Spiritual and sexual, earthy and refined, a woman's voice speaks to women and to the feminine in women and men – of an openness to life, a surrender to the workings of love, and a trust in the Dark Goddesses and their ways of leading us through the dance.

'Potent, seminal, visionary' *Kevin George Brown*

Poetry/Dance ISBN 978-1906900-12-0 £9.99

Words of Re-enchantment: writings on storytelling, myth, and ecological desire
Anthony Nanson

The time-honoured art of storytelling – ancestor of all narrative media – is finding new pathways of relevance in education, consciousness-raising, and the journey of transformation. Storytellers are reinterpreting ancient myths and communicating the new stories we need in our challenging times. This book brings together the best of Anthony Nanson's incisive writings about the ways that story can re-enchant our lives and the world we live in. Grounded in his practice as a storyteller, the essays range from the myths of Arthur, Arcadia, and the voyage west, to true tales of the past, science-fiction visions of the future, and the big questions of politics and spirituality such stories raise. The book contains full texts of exemplar stories and will stimulate the thinking of anyone interested in storytelling or in the use of myth in fiction and film.

'This excellent book is written with a storyteller's cadence and understanding of language. Passionate, fascinating and wise.' *Hamish Fyfe*

Storytelling/Mythology/Environment ISBN 978-1-906900-15-1 £9.99

Tidal Shift: selected poems
Mary Palmer

Knowing her end was near, Mary Palmer worked on her poems, compiling her very best and writing new ones with a feverish intensity. This is the result, published here with her full cooperation and consent. These are poems from the extreme edge and very centre of life – words of light that defy death's shadow with a startling intensity, clarity, and honesty. Containing poems from across Mary's career, selected by Jay Ramsay, *Tidal Shift* is an impressive legacy from a poet of soul and insight.

'She has the courage to confront struggles and sickness, the world's and her own. Unpious but radically spiritual, she stays faithfully questioning right to the end.' *Philip Gross*

Poetry ISBN 978-1-906900-09-0 £9.99

Glossing the Spoils
Charlotte Hussey

Each poem in *Glossing the Spoils* works like an intricate time-travel machine, carrying the reader back to the beginnings of Western European literature. Like an ancient clapper bridge with its unmortared slabs of flat sandstone, these poems step us across the choppy currents of the past 1500 years. Anchored at one end in the deep past and at the other in the turbulent present, they explore interconnections between historical, personal, psychological, and mythic states. Plundering their opening passages from such early texts as *Beowulf*, *The Mabinogion*, and *The Tain*, these glosas address eternal themes of love and war and give voice to the surreal potency of the Western European imagination.

'The author is not only a gifted poet, but also well versed in Celtic mythology. She writes from a spiritual perspective that brings these ancient stories alive and relevant to our world today.' *Abena*

Poetry ISBN 978-1-906900-52-6 £8.99

Exotic Excursions
Anthony Nanson

In these stories Anthony Nanson charts the territory between travel writing and magic realism to confront the exotic and the enigmatic. Here are epiphanies of solitude, twilight and initiation. A lover's true self unveiled by a mountain mist … a memory of the lost land in the western sea … a traveller's surrender to the allure of ancient gods … a quest for primeval beings on the edge of extinction. In transcending the line between the written and the spoken word, between the familiar and the unfamiliar, between the actual and the imagined, these tales send sparks across the gap of desire.

'He is a masterful storyteller, and his prose is delightful to read … His sheer technical ability makes my bones rattle with joy.' *Mimi Thebo*

Fiction/Travel ISBN 987-0-9546137-7-8 £7.99

The Firekeeper's Daughter
Karola Renard

From the vastness of Stone Age Siberia to a minefield in today's Angola, from the black beaches of Iceland to the African savannah and a Jewish-German cemetery, Karola Renard tells thirteen mythic stories of initiation featuring twenty-first-century kelpies, sirens, and holy fools, a river of tears and a girl who dances on fire, a maiden shaman of ice, a witch in a secret garden, Queen Guinevere's magic mirror, and a woman who swallows the moon. The red thread running through them all is a deep faith in life and the need to find truth and meaning even in the greatest of ordeals.

'In her lively and vivid stories, Karola Renard points a finger towards the mythic threads that run through life's initiations.' *Martin Shaw*

Fiction ISBN 978-1-906900-46-5 £9.99

Iona
Mary Palmer

What do you do when you are torn apart by your 'selves'? The pilgrim poet, rebel Mordec and tweedy Aelia set sail for Iona – a thin place, an island on the edge. It's a journey between worlds, back to the roots of their culture. On the Height of Storm they relive a Viking massacre, at Port of the Coracle encounter vipers. They meet Morrighan, a bloodthirsty goddess, and Abbot Dominic with his concubine nuns. There are omens, chants, curses … During her stay Mordec learns that words can heal or destroy, and the poet writes her way out of darkness. A powerful story, celebrating a journey to wholeness, from an accomplished poet.

'Always truthful, this poetry confronts both beauty and ugliness and makes space for light to slip between the two.' *Rose Flint*

Poetry ISBN 978-0-9546137-8-5 £6.99
Spirit of Place Volume 1

The Immanent Moment
Kevan Manwaring

The sound of snow falling on a Somerset hillside, the evanescence of a waterspout on a remote Scottish island, the invisible view from a Welsh mountain, the light on the Grand Canal in Venice, the fire in a Bedouin camel-herder's eyes … These poems consider the little epiphanies of life and capture such fleeting pulses of consciousness in sinuous, euphonic language. A meditation on time, mortality, transience, and place, this collection celebrates the beauty of both the natural and the man-made, the familiar and the exotic, and the interstices and intimacy of love.

Poetry ISBN 978-1-906900-41-0 £8.99

The Fifth Quarter
Richard Selby

The Fifth Quarter is Romney Marsh, as defined by the Revd Richard Harris Barham in *The Ingoldsby Legends*: 'The World, according to the best geographers, is divided into Europe, Asia, Africa, America and Romney Marsh.' It is a place apart, almost another world. This collection of stories and poems explores its ancient and modern landscapes, wonders at its past, and reflects upon its present. Richard Selby has known Romney Marsh all his life. His writing reflects the uniqueness of The Marsh through prose, poetry, and written versions of stories he performs as a storyteller.

Fiction/Poetry ISBN 978-0-9546137-9-2 £9.99
Spirit of Place Volume 2

Mysteries
Chrissy Derbyshire

This enchanting and exquisitely crafted collection by Chrissy Derbyshire will whet your appetite for more from this budding wordsmith. Her short stories interlaced with poems depict chimeras, femmes fatales, mountebanks, absinthe addicts, changelings, derelict warlocks and persons foolhardy enough to stray into the beguiling world of Faerie. Let the sirens' song seduce you into the Underworld …

Fiction/Poetry ISBN 978-1-906900-45-8 £8.99

The Long Woman
Kevan Manwaring

An antiquarian's widow discovers her husband's lost journals and sets out on a journey of remembrance across 1920s England and France, retracing his steps in search of healing and independence. Along alignments of place and memory she meets mystic Dion Fortune, ley-line pioneer Alfred Watkins, and a Sir Arthur Conan Doyle obsessed with the Cottingley Fairies. From Glastonbury to Carnac, she visits the ancient sites that obsessed her husband and, tested by both earthly and unearthly forces, she discovers a power within herself.

'A beautiful book, filled with the quiet of dawn, and the first cool breaths of new life, it reveals how the poignance of real humanity is ever sprinkled with magic.' *Emma Restall Orr*

Fiction ISBN 978-1-906900-44-1 £9.99
The Windsmith Elegy Volume 1

A Dance with Hermes
Lindsay Clarke

In a verse sequence that swoops between wit and ancient wisdom, between the mystical and the mischievous, award-winning novelist Lindsay Clarke elucidates the trickster nature of Hermes, the messenger god of imagination, language, dreams, travel, theft, tweets, and trading floors, who is also the presiding deity of alchemy and the guide of souls into the otherworld. Taking a fresh look at some classical myths, this vivacious dance with Hermes choreographs ways in which, as an archetype of the poetic basis of mind, the sometimes disreputable god remains as provocative as ever in a world that worries – among other things – about losing its iPhone, what happens after death, online scams, and the perplexing condition of its soul.

'Lindsay Clarke's poems wonderfully embody what they describe: the god Hermes, who is comprehensively shown to be just as revelatory and double-dealing in the digital age as he ever was in antiquity.' *Patrick Harpur*

Poetry/Mythology ISBN 978-1906900-43-4 £10.00

Made in the USA
Columbia, SC
11 July 2018